Lecture Notes in Computer Science   12409

More information about this series at http://www.springer.com/series/7408

Qingyang Wang · Yunni Xia ·
Sangeetha Seshadri · Liang-Jie Zhang (Eds.)

Services Computing –
SCC 2020

17th International Conference
Held as Part of the Services Conference Federation, SCF 2020
Honolulu, HI, USA, September 18–20, 2020
Proceedings

Springer

Editors
Qingyang Wang (ID)
Louisana State University
Baton Rouge, LA, USA

Yunni Xia
Chongqing University
Chongqing, China

Sangeetha Seshadri
IBM Almaden Research Center
San Jose, CA, USA

Liang-Jie Zhang (ID)
Kingdee International Software
Group Co. Ltd.
Shenzhen, China

ISSN 0302-9743   ISSN 1611-3349 (electronic)
Lecture Notes in Computer Science
ISBN 978-3-030-59591-3   ISBN 978-3-030-59592-0 (eBook)
https://doi.org/10.1007/978-3-030-59592-0

LNCS Sublibrary: SL2 – Programming and Software Engineering

This Springer imprint is published by the registered company Springer Nature Switzerland AG
The registered company address is: Gewerbestrasse 11, 6330 Cham, Switzerland

Preface

Services account for a major part of the IT industry today. Companies increasingly like to focus on their core expertise area and use IT services to address all their peripheral needs. Services computing is a new science that aims to study and better understand the foundations of this highly popular industry. It covers the science and technology of leveraging computing and information technology to model, create, operate, and manage business services. The International Conference on Services Computing (SCC 2020) contributes to building the pillars of this important science and shaping the future of services computing.

SCC has been a prime international forum for both researchers and industry practitioners to exchange the latest fundamental advances in the state of the art and practice of business modeling, business consulting, solution creation, service delivery, and software architecture design, development, and deployment.

This volume presents the accepted papers for SCC 2020, held as a fully virtual conference, during September 18–20, 2020. For SCC 2020, we accepted eight full papers and two short papers. Each was reviewed and selected by at least three independent members of the SCC 2020 International Program Committee. We are pleased to thank the authors whose submissions and participation made this conference possible. We also want to express our thanks to the Organizing Committee and Program Committee members, for their dedication in helping to organize the conference and reviewing the submissions. We owe special thanks to the keynote speakers for their impressive speeches.

July 2020

Qingyang Wang
Yunni Xia
Sangeetha Seshadri
Liang-Jie Zhang

Organization

General Chair

Lakshmish Ramaswamy   University of Georgia, USA

Program Chairs

Qingyang Wang   Louisiana State University, USA
Yunni Xia   Chongqing University, China
Sangeetha Seshadri   IBM Almaden Research Center, USA

Services Conference Federation (SCF 2020)

General Chairs

Yi Pan   Georgia State University, USA
Samee U. Khan   North Dakota State University, USA
Wu Chou   Vice President of Artificial Intelligence & Software at
    Essenlix Corporation, USA
Ali Arsanjani   Amazon Web Services (AWS), USA

Program Chair

Liang-Jie Zhang   Kingdee International Software Group Co. Ltd., China

Industry Track Chair

Siva Kantamneni   Principal/Partner at Deloitte Consulting, USA

CFO

Min Luo   Georgia Tech, USA

Industry Exhibit and International Affairs Chair

Zhixiong Chen   Mercy College, USA

Operation Committee

Jing Zeng   Yundee Intelligence Co., Ltd, China
Yishuang Ning   Tsinghua University, China
Sheng He   Tsinghua University, China
Yang Liu   Tsinghua University, China

Steering Committee

Calton Pu (Co-chair)	Georgia Tech, USA
Liang-Jie Zhang (Co-chair)	Kingdee International Software Group Co. Ltd., China

SCC 2020 Program Committee

Lizhen Cui	Shandong University, China
Kenneth Fletcher	University of Massachusetts Boston, USA
Pedro Furtado	University of Coimbra, Portugal
Kurt Geihs	University of Kassel, Germany
Alfredo Goldmanm	USP, Brazil
Shigeru Hosono	Tokyo University of Technology, Japan
Shijun Liu	Shandong University, China
Massimo Mecella	Sapienza Università di Roma, Italy
Marcio Oikawa	Federal University of ABC, Brazil
Lukas Rupprecht	IBM Almaden Research Center, USA
Andre Luis Schwerz	Federal University of Technology Paraná, Brazil
Jun Shen	University of Wollongong, Australia
Yang Syu	Academia Sinica, Taiwan
Dingwen Tao	University of Alabama, USA
Yu-Bin Yang	Nanjing University, China
Muhammad Younas	Oxford Brookes University, UK

Conference Sponsor – Services Society

Services Society (S2) is a nonprofit professional organization that has been created to promote worldwide research and technical collaboration in services innovation among academia and industrial professionals. Its members are volunteers from industry and academia with common interests. S2 is registered in the USA as a "501(c) organization," which means that it is an American tax-exempt nonprofit organization. S2 collaborates with other professional organizations to sponsor or co-sponsor conferences and to promote an effective services curriculum in colleges and universities. The S2 initiates and promotes a "Services University" program worldwide to bridge the gap between industrial needs and university instruction.

The services sector accounted for 79.5% of the USA's GDP in 2016. The world's most service-oriented economy, with services sectors accounting for more than 90% of the GDP. S2 has formed 10 Special Interest Groups (SIGs) to support technology and domain specific professional activities:

- Special Interest Group on Web Services (SIG-WS)
- Special Interest Group on Services Computing (SIG-SC)
- Special Interest Group on Services Industry (SIG-SI)
- Special Interest Group on Big Data (SIG-BD)
- Special Interest Group on Cloud Computing (SIG-CLOUD)
- Special Interest Group on Artificial Intelligence (SIG-AI)
- Special Interest Group on Edge Computing (SIG-EC)
- Special Interest Group on Cognitive Computing (SIG-CC)
- Special Interest Group on Blockchain (SIG-BC)
- Special Interest Group on Internet of Things (SIG-IOT)

About the Services Conference Federation (SCF)

As the founding member of the Services Conference Federation (SCF), the First International Conference on Web Services (ICWS 2003) was held in June 2003 in Las Vegas, USA. Meanwhile, the First International Conference on Web Services - Europe 2003 (ICWS-Europe 2003) was held in Germany in October 2003. ICWS-Europe 2003 was an extended event of ICWS 2003, and held in Europe. In 2004, ICWS-Europe was changed to the European Conference on Web Services (ECOWS), which was held in Erfurt, Germany. SCF 2019 was held successfully in San Diego, USA. To celebrate its 18th birthday, SCF 2020 was held virtually during September 18–20, 2020.

In the past 17 years, the ICWS community has expanded from Web engineering innovations to scientific research for the whole services industry. The service delivery platforms have been expanded to mobile platforms, Internet of Things (IoT), cloud computing, and edge computing. The services ecosystem is gradually enabled, value added, and intelligence embedded through enabling technologies such as big data, artificial intelligence (AI), and cognitive computing. In the coming years, all the transactions with multiple parties involved will be transformed to blockchain.

Based on the technology trends and best practices in the field, SCF will continue serving as the conference umbrella's code name for all service-related conferences. SCF 2020 defines the future of New ABCDE (AI, Blockchain, Cloud, big Data, Everything is connected), which enable IoT and enter the 5G for the Services Era. SCF 2020's 10 collocated theme topic conferences all center around "services," while each focusing on exploring different themes (web-based services, cloud-based services, big data-based services, services innovation lifecycle, AI-driven ubiquitous services, blockchain driven trust service-ecosystems, industry-specific services and applications, and emerging service-oriented technologies). SCF includes 10 service-oriented conferences: ICWS, CLOUD, SCC, BigData Congress, AIMS, SERVICES, ICIOT, EDGE, ICCC, and ICBC. The SCF 2020 members are listed as follows:

[1] The International Conference on Web Services (ICWS 2020, http://icws.org/) is the flagship theme-topic conference for Web-based services, featuring Web services modeling, development, publishing, discovery, composition, testing, adaptation, delivery, as well as the latest API standards.

[2] The International Conference on Cloud Computing (CLOUD 2020, http://thecloudcomputing.org/) is the flagship theme-topic conference for modeling, developing, publishing, monitoring, managing, delivering XaaS (Everything as a Service) in the context of various types of cloud environments.

[3] The International Conference on Big Data (BigData 2020, http://bigdatacongress.org/) is the emerging theme-topic conference for the scientific and engineering innovations of big data.

[4] The International Conference on Services Computing (SCC 2020, http://thescc.org/) is the flagship theme-topic conference for services innovation lifecycle that includes enterprise modeling, business consulting, solution creation, services

orchestration, services optimization, services management, services marketing, and business process integration and management.

[5] The International Conference on AI & Mobile Services (AIMS 2020, http://ai1000.org/) is the emerging theme-topic conference for the science and technology of AI, and the development, publication, discovery, orchestration, invocation, testing, delivery, and certification of AI-enabled services and mobile applications.

[6] The World Congress on Services (SERVICES 2020, http://servicescongress.org/) focuses on emerging service-oriented technologies and the industry-specific services and solutions.

[7] The International Conference on Cognitive Computing (ICCC 2020, http://thecognitivecomputing.org/) focuses on the Sensing Intelligence (SI) as a Service (SIaaS) which makes systems listen, speak, see, smell, taste, understand, interact, and walk in the context of scientific research and engineering solutions.

[8] The International Conference on Internet of Things (ICIOT 2020, http://iciot.org/) focuses on the creation of IoT technologies and development of IOT services.

[9] The International Conference on Edge Computing (EDGE 2020, http://theedgecomputing.org/) focuses on the state of the art and practice of edge computing including but not limited to localized resource sharing, connections with the cloud, and 5G devices and applications.

[10] The International Conference on Blockchain (ICBC 2020, http://blockchain1000.org/) concentrates on blockchain-based services and enabling technologies.

Some highlights of SCF 2020 are shown below:

- **Bigger Platform:** The 10 collocated conferences (SCF 2020) are sponsored by the Services Society (S2) which is the world-leading nonprofit organization (501 c(3)) dedicated to serving more than 30,000 worldwide services computing researchers and practitioners. Bigger platform means bigger opportunities to all volunteers, authors, and participants. Meanwhile, Springer sponsors the Best Paper Awards and other professional activities. All the 10 conference proceedings of SCF 2020 have been published by Springer and indexed in ISI Conference Proceedings Citation Index (included in Web of Science), Engineering Index EI (Compendex and Inspec databases), DBLP, Google Scholar, IO-Port, MathSciNet, Scopus, and ZBlMath.

- **Brighter Future:** While celebrating the 2020 version of ICWS, SCF 2020 highlights the Third International Conference on Blockchain (ICBC 2020) to build the fundamental infrastructure for enabling secure and trusted service ecosystems. It will also lead our community members to create their own brighter future.

- **Better Model:** SCF 2020 continues to leverage the invented Conference Blockchain Model (CBM) to innovate the organizing practices for all the 10 theme conferences.

Contents

Research Track

QoS Time Series Modeling and Forecasting for Web Services: A Comprehensive Survey of Subsequent Applications and Experimental Configurations

Yang Syu[(⊠)] and Chien-Min Wang

Institute of Information Science, Academia Sinica, Taipei City, Taiwan (R.O.C.)
{yangsyu, cmwang}@iis.sinica.edu.tw

Abstract. Time-aware (time series-based) Web service QoS modeling and forecasting have been investigated and addressed for over a decade and a large number of studies and approaches have been produced. However, these existing efforts lack a comprehensive and detailed review that profoundly and systematically organizes, analyzes, and discusses this body of work. Thus, to fill this gap, the authors offered the paper *QoS Time Series Modeling and Forecasting for Web Services: A Comprehensive Survey*, in which four essential research concerns of this area, namely, problems, approaches, performance measures, and QoS datasets, have been recognized and reviewed in detail. However, aside from these essential research concerns, we also identified two optional research concerns from the current studies, namely, the subsequent applications and experimental configurations. Due to space restrictions, these two optional research concerns were only briefly mentioned in the above survey article, and thus, in this supplementary paper, the authors thoroughly present and review these two optional research concerns.

The primary purpose of performing QoS time series modeling and forecasting is to obtain accurate future QoS estimations for subsequent usage (application), such as QoS-aware service composition and proactive service replacement for SLA/QoS management. Therefore, in the section addressing the first optional research concern, the application of each surveyed study is identified first, and then these current applications are introduced in detail. However, to comprehensively and rigorously observe and evaluate the performance of a proposed or employed approach under different conditions, a set of configuration settings must be varied to run experimentation. Thus, in the second part of this paper, we first define and discuss the identified experimental configuration parameters in this research area and then list the parameters and settings that have been considered in each surveyed study.

Keywords: Quality of service · Web services · Time series modeling and forecasting · Time-aware dynamic attributes

© Springer Nature Switzerland AG 2020
Q. Wang et al. (Eds.): SCC 2020, LNCS 12409, pp. 3–19, 2020.
https://doi.org/10.1007/978-3-030-59592-0_1

1   Introduction

In services computing research, the estimation and prediction of the dynamic QoS attributes of Web/cloud services have been widely considered and investigated, and a large body of research addresses this long-standing issue. From the existing studies and approaches, we observe that in terms of the assumed and studied problem specifications, there are two major research branches in this area that are divided by considering disparate factors causing dynamic QoS values (i.e., consumer-aware and time-aware QoS prediction). The latter type of QoS prediction is also called time series-based QoS forecasting or QoS time series prediction for Web services because, in essence, it is a type and application of time series forecasting that concentrates on employing the historical QoS observations of a target (i.e., a dynamic QoS property of a service) to generate a forecast to predict the target's future values. This research topic has been studied for approximately a decade [1], and significant research results have been produced and accumulated; however, based on our observations and investigations, the current research on this topic lacks a referable survey to review, structure, and compare these existing research works. Thus, in the 2018 International Conference on Services Computing (SCC 2018), the authors published an initial paper [1] surveying Web service QoS (WS QoS) time series modeling and forecasting research. In this preliminary survey, based on an overview table organizing and demonstrating the characteristics of the surveyed papers in a proposed structure, we discuss and explore these reviewed studies from several different aspects; however, a shortcoming of this preliminary survey is its insufficient depth and completeness. To fix the problem, we subsequently offered an extended journal survey article [2] comprehensively reviewing the targeted topic in detail. In this journal paper, for WS QoS time series modeling and forecasting research, we identify four essential research concerns, namely, considered problems, proposed or employed approaches, adopted performance measures, and employed QoS datasets, and two optional research concerns: subsequent applications and experimental configurations. In [2], the considered and reviewed studies were thoroughly analyzed, organized, and compared in terms of the four essential research concerns; however, due to the restricted space, the two optional research concerns are only briefly mentioned. Thus, this paper tries to complete this section of the earlier survey for Web service QoS time series modeling and forecasting research by presenting the content of these two optional research concerns in detail.

Although we identify and consider both experimental configurations and subsequent applications as two optional research concerns of WS QoS time series modeling and forecasting in [2], this does not mean that they are insignificant or ignorable in this research area; instead, they are also very important to the topic, but some of the reviewed studies simply did not consider one or both of these two research concerns for various reasons, such as a lack of space for their presentation, a lack of awareness of their importance, or an exclusive concentration on the WS QoS modeling and forecasting problem. Below, as a motivation behind this survey, we briefly explain the importance of these two optional research concerns in the targeted and reviewed research field. The main goal of WS QoS time series modeling and forecasting is to obtain a sequence of estimated future QoS values for certain subsequent usage; in other words, without a specific or concrete subsequent application, simply having an accurate QoS forecasting approach is meaningless and useless; there must be some consumers consuming and exploiting these QoS predictions in order to make them valuable and useful. Furthermore, some reviewed studies also employ or consider the performance of a subsequent application (using a QoS forecasting approach as the source of future QoS values) as one of the measures for judging the accuracy and applicability of a proposed/evaluated QoS forecasting approach, such as [3–5]; we believe that assessing a WS QoS prediction approach in this way can more realistically and accurately reflect its applicability, reliability, and performance because it is used and evaluated in a real-world context. On the other hand, in both research and practice, one common way to fully test and comprehensively know the performance of an employed or proposed approach is to feed or exercise the approach using different problem instances (e.g., a number of disparate sequences of historic QoS observations) and then observe and calculate the results of these different problem instances. However, beyond varying problem instances, another common element/ dimension to vary in order to insightfully and rigorously assess an approach is the problem parameters/experimental conditions (e.g., the size of available historic QoS observations). For the experimental outcomes and conclusion to be convincing and informative, an approach or a set of approaches must be evaluated under a variety of different situations/conditions for the same problem instance; for example, an approach may be tested with a poor, medium, and rich amount of training/learning materials so that the performance of the approach under different conditions can be known, and then more precise and informed decision and profound observation can be made.

Last, we discuss the content and contribution of this paper. Basically, as a supplement to [2], the basic contribution, purpose, and possible usage of this survey paper is the same as those described in [2]. First, we review current applications of WS QoS time series modeling and forecasting and how they exploit QoS predictions in Sect. 2; however, beyond realizing existing applications, a hope is to inspire the proposal and development of more applications taking advantage of time-aware QoS forecasting approaches in this research area. Subsequently, Sect. 3 fully reviews and introduces the experimental considerations/configuration parameters appearing and considered in the surveyed papers; an experimenter can refer to them to design his/her experiments, avoiding missing any of the varied and tested properties/conditions. Finally, we conclude this paper in Sect. 4.

2 Subsequent Application

In this section, we first overview what applications have been considered in each of the reviewed studies in Table 1, and then these disparate applications are introduced and discussed in detail one after another.

First, Table 1 lists the surveyed studies ordered by the year of their publication; more general information on these studies, including their publication type and venue (journal/conference), study type (research approach/empirical comparison), and targeted time-aware dynamic QoS attribute (e.g., response time) can be found in [2]. In addition to this general information (shown in the first two columns of Table 1), the table also enumerates the application assumed, adopted, or combined in each reviewed study in its third column. Furthermore, in the fourth column of the table, we also identify whether an application in a study (if any) has been realistically implemented/ simulated. In some of the reviewed papers, such as [6–8], the authors only briefly mention in a few sentences where their QoS forecasting approach could be used but do not offer a practical implementation/simulation or theoretical process/framework/ discussion of the mentioned application; in this survey, we consider such studies as having no application. For those studies that have an application in the third column of Table 1, we further divide them into two classes in the fourth column of the table; the first class indicates if the application of a study has been concretely implemented or simulated, and the other contains those that the authors only theoretically discuss, define, or propose in their paper without any realistic implementation or simulation.

Table 1. The reviewed Web service QoS time series modeling and forecasting studies and their considered/combined subsequent applications.

Authors	Year published	Application	Implementation/Simulation
Syu et al. [9]	2019	None	None
Ding et al. [3]	2018	Cloud service recommendation based on the ranking of aggregated QoS predictions	Yes
Syu et al. [10]	2017	None	None
Zhang et al. [11]	2017	None	None
Fanjiang et al. [8]	2016	None	None
Ye et al. [12]	2016	Long-term QoS-aware service composition/selection	Yes
Nourikhah et al. [13]	2015	None	None
Rehman et al. [14]	2014	None	None
Leitner et al. [15]	2013	SLA violation prediction	The implementation of the proposed framework did not include its application phase
YunNi et al. [4]	2013	Dependability prediction for composite services	Yes
Amin et al. (a). [16]	2012	SLA violation prediction	Yes
Amin et al. (b). [6]	2012	None	None
Li et al. [5]	2012	Service recommendation based on the ranking of the aggregations of trustworthiness predictions and functionality similarity	Yes
Senivongse et al. [17]	2011	QoS-aware service composition/selection	Yes
Solomon et al. [18]	2011	Business process (management) performance prediction	Yes
Zadeh et al. [19]	2010	QoS monitoring	A theoretical framework for QoS monitoring
Cavallo et al. [20]	2010	SLA violation prediction	Yes
Godse et al. [21]	2010	QoS-aware service composition/selection	A theoretical QoS-aware service selection process
Li et al. [7]	2010	None	None
Mu et al. [22]	2009	QoS-aware service composition/selection	Yes
Malak et al. [23]	2009	QoS-aware service composition/selection and SLA violation prediction	An agent-based theoretical architecture for the management of QoS

Below, we introduce and discusses the six disparate applications appearing in the third column of Table 1 in detail, including how they use and benefit from WS QoS time series modeling and forecasting approaches and why they want to integrate such approaches with their application.

QoS-Aware Service Composition/Selection. As can be seen in Table 1, this is the most common application in the reviewed papers (in five different studies [12, 17, 21–23]), probably because in both services computing and Web service research, service composition/selection has been one of the most widely studied and fertile research topic for a very long time. In industry, modern software engineers often integrate/compose multiple existing Web services to rapidly obtain a required software application or system (rather than creating it from scratch), and developing software applications/systems in this way has already become quite prevalent in practice. In research, how-ever, the focus of investigators is on automating the entire composition process (such as those QoS-aware service composition applications listed in Table 1). A more detailed introduction and definition of automated service composition/selection can be found in [24]). When performing service composition/selection, there are usually multiple con-siderations and conditions that must be satisfied or obeyed, including both the functional and nonfunctional requirements of the requester. Among these different functional/nonfunctional concerns, based on our investigations to date, QoS is the most widely considered and well-studied nonfunctional properties in research [25]. In QoS-aware service composition/selection, the main goal is to optimize the overall QoS performance of a composed composite service, and because a composite service consists of multiple component services, its overall QoS value is actually determined by the QoS values of its component services using a set of QoS aggregation rules specifically designed for dif-ferent flow structures and disparate types of QoS attributes. Thus, when performing QoS-aware composition/selection, the QoS information for the available component services must be known and would be identified by an automatic composition/selection approach. In convention, such QoS information for Web services is provided and published by their providers, and traditional composition/selection approaches just directly accept and rely on this static QoS data to perform their QoS calculations and optimization. In the real world, however, the actual values of time-aware dynamic WS QoS attributes constantly vary over time, and thus, the static QoS information offered by services providers is inaccurate, and subsequently, the composition/selection results based on such unrealistic QoS data are also be incorrect or inappropriate. To improve this deficiency, the researchers reviewed in Table 1 try to employ a WS QoS time series forecasting approach as the source of their QoS information, and then they perform service composition/selection based on the predicted dynamic QoS values of available compo-nent services.

Concentrating on this application, the QoS-aware service composition/selection performed/assumed in the reviewed studies actually varies in terms of the problem specification and considerations. For example, in [12], the authors design a forecasting approach capable of performing long-term, multiple step-ahead (i.e., a forecasting horizon larger than one) QoS time series predictions, and when performing their QoS-aware composition/selection, the considered QoS values are not only those for the next time point/period (the assumption made in most of the reviewed studies) but also those at multiple future consecutive time points/periods. The authors of [12] consider that cloud services are mostly rented and used over a long period of time, and thus, the future long-term QoS performance must be known in advance and considered when performing cloud service composition/selection. As another example, the assumption made in [17] is that some component services are able to satisfy/implement multiple abstract activities in a workflow (the convention is that the functionality of each concrete service can fulfill only one specific abstract activity). Even with these differences in the assumed and addressed QoS-aware service composition/selection problems, however, the commonality of these studies is that they all employ a time-aware QoS prediction approach to provide their time-aware dynamic QoS information, seeking more reliable and precise composition/selection outcomes.

SLA Violation Prediction. Based on the table, this is the second most common application in the reviewed studies (considered in four different papers [15, 16, 20, 23]). Since Web/cloud services are usually external software components (their access mostly must through Internet), typically, a service consumer has a contract with each of its service providers to ensure that the nonfunctional performance of the exploited external services reaches or surpasses a pre-negotiated minimal level; this contract is usually called a service level agreement (SLA). A conventional SLA contract instance consists of multiple service level objectives (SLOs), each including both a minimum threshold and a penalty for each specific QoS attribute. An SLO instance, for example, could be that the response time of a service must be within a certain duration (e.g., 0.1 s), and the penalty could be that if a service provider violates this objective (i.e., an SLA violation instance), the usage fee paid to the service provider would be reduced (e.g., only 50% of the original price). A further introduction to SLA can be found in [15]. From the perspective of service consumers, an SLA violation is definitely to be avoided because it damages and decreases the reliability and stability of their service-based system. In addition, service providers want to avoid SLA violations as completely as possible because violations reduce their revenues and damage their reputations. To deal with service violations, currently, there are two categories of approaches: conventional reactive service substitution and innovative proactive service replacement. The former type of approach constantly monitors the real-time QoS values of running services, and when an SLA/SLO violation is detected during runtime, the approach automatically and dynamically replaces the problematic service with another QoS-appropriate, functionality-equivalent service to maintain the enacted SLA contract. However, the shortcoming of this approach is that the users of an SLA-violated system will experience violated QoS until the runtime substitution is made. To overcome this deficiency, proactive service replacement has been proposed and studied in research. This technique depends on SLA violation prediction to anticipate future SLA violation, and before the violation actually occurs, the predicted QoS/SLA-violated service would be proactively replaced to prevent the violation from happening. In this way, the users do not need to tolerate or suffer from any inconvenience or performance decrease caused by QoS/SLA violation at all.

The key to proactive service replacement is the accuracy of the SLA violation prediction; if a violation is wrongly anticipated or missed, an unnecessary service substitution would be conducted or the prevention of a violation will fail. Currently, there are two types of approaches for SLA violation prediction, direct and indirect prediction, and all the reviewed SLA violation prediction applications in Table 1 belong to the latter type, in which the future QoS value of a time-aware dynamic QoS attribute is first estimated using a WS QoS time series modeling and forecasting approach, and then this forecasted value is compared with the threshold specified in the corresponding SLO to determine whether a violation is going to occur or not.

Service Recommendation. Due to their popularity, prevalence, and convenience, currently, there are many Web/cloud services available on the Web or within service registries, and because of this enormous number of services, manually selecting an appropriate and required service can be a difficult and time-consuming task. In this case, service recommendation can help service consumers to automatically and quickly choose the most suitable option from a large set of candidate services by ranking them based on the adopted selection criteria. When conducting such recommendation/selection, currently, aside from functionality, the most widely considered nonfunctional criterion for services is QoS. When performing computation for the recommendation, the recommended service would actually be used in the future, but most traditional recommendation approaches only refer to the static QoS information offered by service providers without considering the variation and volatility of time-aware dynamic QoS attributes. Thus, offering recommendations based on present or static QoS data would result in an incorrect ranking of services and potentially the subsequent inappropriate selection and recommendation of a service. To fix this issue, the service recommendation applications reviewed in Table 1 exploit a time-aware WS QoS forecasting approach to obtain the estimated future QoS values of their candidate services and then perform recommendation/ranking based on these predicted QoS values. Finally, a difference between the reviewed service recommendation applications is their considered criterion; when performing ranking, [3] considers only the QoS properties of candidate services, but [5] takes both the predicted trustworthiness and the service's similarity in functionality to the specified requirements into account.

Dependability Prediction. Calculation of the dependability of a software system has been a long-standing research issue. In general, the dependability of a software system depends on that of its components/modules and its architecture. Similarly, because a service-based system (a service composition/composite service instance) consists of multiple component services, its overall dependability is determined by the dependability of its component services and the composition structures of these component services (which can be viewed as the architecture of the composite service). Unlike traditional software systems, whose components probably all run on the same machine or in the same internal environment, leading to relatively stable and controllable dependability performance, service-oriented systems usually integrate and use external services on the Internet, which causes the overall dependability of such systems to vary largely over time depending on network traffic and the conditions of service providers (this explains why the prediction of dependability for service composition is required).

As mentioned in [4], software dependability is an abstract term, and a number of different definitions exist. In the reviewed application in [4], the authors consider process-normal-completion-probability as the metric for the dependability of a service. As a time-aware dynamic QoS attribute, the actual value of the process-normal-completion-probability of a service changes constantly; thus, to predict the overall dependability of a composite service, the process-normal-completion-probability values of its component services must be forecasted first using a QoS time series modeling and forecasting approach, and then these estimated individual dependability values need to be aggregated based on the workflow structures of the composite service. In [4], both the dependability prediction approach for component services and a set of dependability aggregation rules defined for different composition/workflow structures are proposed and developed by the authors.

Business Process Performance Prediction. A business process comprises both a set of activities that can be implemented or fulfilled by Web services and a logical sequence that structures those activities in a specific order of execution, and one of the main purposes of business process management (BPM) is to measure and ensure the key performance indicators (KPIs) when running business process instances during runtime. In [17], the authors need to know the future KPI values of a business process (BP) instance managed by their developed BPM framework. To do so, the authors first develop a simulator capable of computing and simulating the overall KPI values of a BP instance based on the KPI performance of its components (in [17], a BP instance is concretized by a set of Web services, and thus, the KPI performance of BP components is actually the QoS values of those Web services); however, to calculate and simulate future KPI values for a BP instance, the simulator requires component services' future QoS values instead of the current measured QoS values or statistical QoS information offered by service providers (with current or static QoS data, the simulator can only produce current KPI simulation rather than its future estimation). To addressed this problem, the authors employ the outputs of WS QoS time series modeling and forecasting approaches as the inputs of their developed BP KPI simulator; in this way, with the predicted QoS values, the future KPI performance of a BP instance can be simulated and obtained.

QoS Monitoring. Because Web/cloud services are mostly external components, to observe and know their real QoS values, their real-time performance must somehow be constantly measured and recorded. Such dynamic QoS information is necessary to perform subsequent QoS-based actions (such as the detection of an SLA violation as discussed above). In practice, such task is usually done by a QoS monitoring infrastructure or mechanism; however, performing QoS monitoring is a heavy burden on all the participants, including service consumers, providers, and the network environment. In terms of service consumers, for example, some services may not be free for access, and a service consumer need to periodically send a request to each of the monitored services. As another example, service providers running services could receive a large number of detective service requests, which impose a heavy load on their machines and could lead measured QoS values to become unrealistic and imprecise because the limited computing resources of service providers are shared by many monitoring requests (e.g., causing slower response time). Thus, to relieve the heavy burden placed on these service participants and address the problem (distorted measurement of QoS values), the authors of [19] propose using QoS time series forecasting to estimate and obtain QoS values rather than gathering them by truly invoking monitored services. In this way, a current QoS value is produced by employing a sequence of historical QoS observations and exercising a time-aware QoS prediction model, and no additional QoS monitoring action (e.g., sending and processing detective service requests) is required.

Despite these different usages, the commonality of these applications is that they all use WS QoS time series modeling and forecasting approaches as the source of the values of the focal time-aware dynamic QoS attributes in order to enhance (QoS-aware service composition/selection and recommendation), relieve (QoS monitoring), and achieve (SLA violation prediction, dependability prediction, and business process performance prediction) their applications.

3 Experimental Configurations

This section reviews different experimental configuration settings (parameters) that have been adopted, varied, and experimented with in the surveyed papers. From the reviewed studies, we have identified and categorized three different types of experimental configuration settings, *problem-based*, *approach-specific*, and *application-related* variations of experimentation, as listed in Table 2. First, problem-based configuration parameters (experimental variations) are those that originate from WS QoS time series modeling and the forecasting problem itself. More specifically, they are the varying factors in the specification and definition of the targeted research problem. In general, since such configuration settings are based on the studied problem, they are common to all studies focusing on this problem (namely, they all should be considered and varied in the experiments of the reviewed studies); however, this is not the case in the current research, as noted in the second column of Table 2 and discussed in Sect. 3.1. The second recognized type of configuration settings is approach specific. As indicated by its name, such configuration settings are approach dependent, and because the time-aware (time series-based) QoS modeling and forecasting approaches considered or proposed in each study are not the same, approach-specific configuration settings are not common to all the reviewed studies (but in theory, they are common to those studies adopting the same QoS time series prediction approach). In the reviewed studies, most of the identified and varied approach-specific configuration settings are the internal parameters of the prediction approach, as described in Sect. 3.2. Finally, application configuration settings are those that are related to the subsequent application considered in the study rather than to QoS time series modeling and the forecasting problem or approach (therefore, this type of configuration setting is also not common to all the reviewed studies but can be common to those studies integrating or combining the same subsequent application). By varying such configuration parameters, the experimenters can observe and assess both the performance and the reaction of the subsequent application (directly) and the employed QoS forecasting approach (indirectly). We review and discuss this last type of configuration settings in Sect. 3.3.

Table 2. The reviewed studies and their considered experimental configuration settings (parameters).

Authors	Problem based	Approach specific	Application related
Syu et al. [9]	The number of QoS observations for training, the number of QoS observations for testing, and the granularity of time of QoS observations	None	None
Ding et al. [3]	The density of QoS observations (of a QoS time series) for training	The number of similar users considered for filling missing historical QoS entries	The number of ranked services (top-k) in a service recommendation
Syu et al. [10]	None	None	None
Zhang et al. [11]	The size of the QoS forecasting horizon (N-step-ahead prediction)	The dimension of phase space reconstruction and univariate-based vs. multivariate-based QoS forecasting	None
Fanjiang et al. [8]	None	None	None
Ye et al. [12]	The number of QoS observations for training	None	The number of retrieved service compositions
Nourikhah et al. [13]	The size of the QoS forecasting horizon	None	None
Rehman et al. [14]	None	None	None
Leitner et al. [15]	The number of QoS observations for training	None	None
YunNi et al. [4]	None	None	None
Amin et al. (a). [16]	None	None	None
Amin et al. (b). [6]	The number of QoS observations for training	None	None
Li et al. [5]	None	None	The number of ranked services (top-k) in a service recommendation
Senivongse et al. [17]	None	None	None
Solomon et al. [18]	None	None	None
Zadeh et al. [19]	None	None	None
Cavallo et al. [20]	The granularity of time of QoS observations	None	None
Godse et al. [21]	None	None	None
Li et al. [7]	The number of QoS observations for training	None	None
Mu et al. [22]	None	None	The number of candidate services for an abstract activity in a service composition
Malak et al. [23]	None	None	None

3.1 Problem-Based Experimental Configuration Setting

Below, sequentially, we first review the five identified problem-based experimental configuration parameters, and then a general discussion on them is offered, including a discussion of what is lacking in the current studies and their experiments.

The Number of QoS Observations for Training. As shown in Table 2, this is the most widely considered and experimented with configuration setting in the reviewed research. In the targeted research problem, this experimental parameter determines how many historical QoS observations (i.e., available training/learning materials) in a QoS time series modeling and forecasting problem instance are available for the adopted or compared time-aware QoS prediction approaches. In research, such as in many machine learning problems and time series forecasting studies, this experimental parameter has been widely considered and tested because it is quite intuitive for researchers to know and wonder about the performance and cost of an approach based on different amounts of available resources (i.e., changing the value of this experimental parameter to see the relationship between available materials and resulting performance/cost). In the experiments of the reviewed studies, this parameter has been varied to observe its impact on modeling/forecasting accuracy and the time to generate a QoS predictor. The common experimental result across the studies is that prediction accuracy does improve along with more training/learning resources; however, using more QoS observations in the training phase of an approach also causes a longer generation time for predictions (i.e., higher cost).

The Number of QoS Observations for Testing. This parameter determines how many QoS values at consecutive multiple future time points could be predicted by using the same QoS predictor (namely, how long a testing QoS time series is). Based on our investigation, in this research area, most of the reviewed studies adopt off-line, single predictor-based QoS time series forecasting, which means that a generated QoS predictor would be used continuously for multiple QoS predictions without any updating or regeneration of the predictor (except for [3], in which the authors consider online QoS forecasting, and thus, their QoS predictor is revised each time a newly detected QoS observation is available). In other words, the larger the value of this experimental parameter is, the further into the future the predictor will be employed for the QoS predictions (during which, over time, its internal data generation process may become increasingly different from that implied in the training/learning materials of the employed predictor). Among the reviewed studies, only the one presented in [9] has considered and varied this experimental parameter, and their conclusion to this point is that this parameter does influence the forecasting accuracy, and the impact could be both positive and negative (for a detailed discussion, the readers can refer to the tenth paragraph of Sect. 7 of [9]).

The Granularity of Time of QoS Observations. The granularity of time of a time series depends on how often the data sampling is performed, such as hourly, daily, weekly, or monthly (i.e., the interval/distance between two consecutive sampling time points). In our problem context, coarser granularity of time means that a one-step-ahead QoS prediction is for farther in the future, such as a future QoS value for the next hour compared to one for the next day; thus, a common intuition is that the forecasting difficulty will increase along with the adopted granularity of time because it is more difficult to predict farther into the future (for example, forecasting one hour later is much easier than forecasting one week later). Among the reviewed studies, only the authors of [9] [20] have varied this experimental configuration setting to see its impact on forecasting accuracy; however, the authors of [20] only report their hourly based experimental results in the paper (another set of experiments were performed on daily based QoS time series), and thus, there is no way to compare the accuracy of hourly based and daily based QoS forecasting in this case (i.e., unable to observe the influence of the granularity of time). On the other hand, surprisingly, the empirical results demonstrated in [9] violate the abovementioned intuition that coarser-grained granularity for time may yield more accurate QoS forecasting performance. More specifically, based on the experimental data shown in [9], there is a turning point for the granularity of time; before that point, the experimental results match the intuition, but after surpassing it, greater granularity of time leads to more precise QoS prediction.

The Density of QoS Observations for Training. Except for [3], a common assumption implicitly made in the reviewed papers is that all the historical QoS observations of a predicted target are completely available. However, in the real world, such an assumption may not always hold, and missing past QoS values do exist (namely, QoS records are intermittent in a training QoS time series). In [3], the authors consider and address this issue, proposing to employ the historical QoS records of a set of similar service consumers at the same past time point to estimate and fill in the missing QoS values. Afterwards, with the filled-in QoS time series, a predictor is generated to perform subsequent time-aware QoS prediction. Because in this case, the QoS values contained in the training/learning materials are not all real observations, the density and precision of these estimated QoS values will influence the quality of the generated predictor (it is unlikely or very difficult to fit a precise predictor with a sequence of deviated data). In [3], the authors vary the value of the density of the missing QoS observations to see its impact on the accuracy of subsequent WS QoS time series forecasting, and they find that the lower the density of the missing QoS values (i.e., the more real QoS observations available), the better the QoS time series forecasting performance.

The Size of the QoS Forecasting Horizon. This experimental configuration setting determines how many QoS values at consecutive multiple future time points for a targeted QoS attribute would be forecasted in a single prediction. For this consideration, most of the reviewed studies perform and adopt the most basic setting, namely, one-step-ahead forecasting (the size of forecasting horizon is one). However, in some contexts, such as the long-term rental of cloud services considered in [12], a number of future QoS values at multiple later time points need to be known in the present to make an informative long-term decision, and in this case, multiple/N-step-ahead predictions (in which the size of the forecasting horizon is larger than one) must be performed. In most of the reviewed studies (including the papers focusing on both one-step-ahead and multiple/N-step-ahead predictions), the authors set only a fixed value for this configuration parameter to perform their experiments, and thus, they are unable to know the relationship between forecasting accuracy and the size of forecasting horizon through these experiments. In the surveyed studies, the authors of [11, 13] have varied the value of this experimental configuration parameter to see its impact on prediction errors, and their experimental results demonstrate that forecasting errors increase (i.e., worse accuracy) when the stepping number becomes larger.

From the existing studies, we have identified five common factors varied for the targeted and studied problem. In theory, for the experimentation and evaluation of a study to be complete and convincing, each of the first three factors should be independently varied and tested in an experiment to observe and realize its influence on (its relationship with) the resulting performance and cost. However, as demonstrated in the second column of Table 2, many of the surveyed papers actually did not consider any of these factors in their experiments, and most of the other studies only adopt and test one such configuration parameter, which we consider to be one of the major insufficiencies and issues in the current research in this area (namely, the design of the experimentation of these studies is poor in terms of its coverage of different problem conditions). Regarding the last two problem-based experimental configuration settings, the fourth should be included and varied if the verified approach is capable of dealing with missing historical QoS observations in design, and the last must be considered when performing multiple (N-step-ahead) QoS time series forecasts in a single prediction.

Finally, a problem-based experimental configuration setting that is never varied and tested in current studies is the frequency of retraining/updating a QoS time series predictor. In [11], the predictor is updated each time it receives a new QoS observation, and in the other studies, the same predictor would be used for the entire prediction problem instance (i.e., the whole testing QoS time series). We consider that the above two situations are two extreme cases (namely, updating each time and never revising/regenerating), and a suitable and cost-efficient updating/retraining frequency between these two extreme cases for an encountered problem instance should be studied and determined (such as varying and testing different frequencies to see the resulting forecasting accuracy and total consumed time). For an optimal frequency or a balance point between accuracy and time, a possible research direction is to analyze the pattern and cycle of the change in the internal (data generation) process of the QoS time series. For example, if the internal process does not change, the predictor generated for the process is not obsolete and can still be used for subsequent QoS time series forecasting; however, if the process changes, a new predictor must be obtained using the most recent QoS observations (i.e., QoS data generated by the new internal process) to replace the old predictor (similar to those done in [26]).

3.2   Approach-Specific Experimental Configuration Settings

The experimental configuration settings reviewed and identified in this section are approach dependent/specific; thus, we only briefly review them because they are not common to the entire research area and all the surveyed studies.

The Number of Considered Similar Users for Filling in Missing Historical QoS Entries. The authors of [3] employ the historical QoS records of a set of similar service users (data) and a collaborative filtering-based method (approach) to estimate the missing QoS values at past time points for a target user. In their experiments, the number of included similar users is varied from 2 to 30 to see its influence on the estimation of missing past QoS values and application (service recommendation) performance. Their experimental results and discussion conclude that considering the top-5 most similar users (their QoS records) is the best option, and considering either fewer or more similar users may lead to worse outcomes (i.e., higher errors).

The Dimension of Phase Space Reconstruction. Phase space reconstruction is the last step for the data preprocessing used in the QoS time series forecasting approach proposed in [11]. In their experiments, the authors have varied the dimension value of the phase space reconstruction and fixed the other parameter (i.e., step number) to observe their empirical results (demonstrated in the form of a comparison between a sequence of prediction values and the corresponding actual QoS observations). However, in the paper, the authors did not explicitly discuss the effect of different dimension values on forecasting accuracy, and it is difficult to figure this out it based on their experimental results.

Univariate-Based vs. Multivariate-Based QoS Forecasting. The time-aware QoS prediction approach proposed in [11] is capable of performing both univariate-based and multivariate-based QoS time series forecasting (i.e., an internal configuration setting of this approach allows a choice of the kind of prediction), and the authors have an empirical comparison for their prediction accuracy. The experimental results indicate that for one-step-ahead forecasting (i.e., the size of forecasting horizon is one), the univariate version of the approach is sufficient in terms of forecasting accuracy; however, for multiple-step-ahead QoS prediction (the size of forecasting horizon is larger than one), the multivariate-based approach is better than univariate one because the authors consider multivariate QoS observations to contain more useful information.

3.3   Application-Related Experimental Configuration Setting

This section contains experimental configuration settings/parameters that are related to the identified applications of WS QoS time series modeling and forecasting approaches (i.e., those reviewed in Sect. 2); in experimentation, these values/settings have been varied to see their impact on the resulting performance (of the application).

The Number of Ranked Services (top-k) in a Service Recommendation. In [3, 5], their subsequent application is service recommendation (as reviewed in Table 1), and they both adopt discounted cumulative gain (DCG, for which a higher resulting value indicates better performance) to assess the ranking accuracy of the k recommended services (i.e., the top-k candidates) in a recommendation that is based on the forecasted QoS values. In their experimentation, the value of k is varied, and the experimental results in [5] and the outcomes of response time-based experiments in [3] show that the higher the value of k is (i.e., the more ranked and recommended services in a recommendation), the better the application performance is as measured in DCG; however, this is not the case for the throughput-based service recommendation experiments reported in [3], in which higher values of k cause lower (worse) DCG values. Thus, based on these empirical investigations, the configuration settings of a QoS-based application should take the type and feature of time-aware dynamic QoS attributes into account.

The Number of Retrieved Service Compositions. The application of the QoS time series forecasting approach in [12] is service composition. With the application approach of [12], for each service composition request, a set of service compositions based on the predicted QoS values are returned. In their experiments, the authors have varied the number of returned service compositions each time to see the impact on application performance measured in three different metrics (i.e., accuracy, F-measure, and fall-out), and their empirical results demonstrate that overall, the greater the number of retrieved composition instances for a request, the worse the measured application performance.

The Number of Candidate Services for an Abstract Activity in a Service Composition. In service composition/selection research, a widely studied and tested basic varying factor is the number of available service candidates for each abstract activity contained in a workflow. Obviously, the higher the number of candidate services, the more difficult the composition/selection problem is because there are more possible composition instances (i.e., a larger solution space). However, among the reviewed studies that consider service composition/selection as their subsequent application, only the authors of [22] have varied this application parameter from 5 to 30 in their experiments to see its influence on computational cost; reasonably, their experimental results indicate that the larger the number of available candidate services is, the higher the cost.

Finally, we briefly mention an experimental configuration setting that did not belong to the above three types. In Sect. 2, we explain how forecasted QoS values are used by different subsequent applications (i.e., how a QoS forecasting approach and an application are combined and used together), and their pattern of combination is the same for each application (i.e., how they are combined is never varied and compared). However, an exception found in the reviewed studies is [18], in which three different combination patterns have been empirically tested and compared in their experimentation to find the best one.

4 Conclusion

In this paper, we review two concerns of WS QoS time series modeling and forecasting research, namely, its subsequent application and the experimental configuration settings considered. In the paper, we have identified and introduced five different applications in current research that have been integrated and tested with a time-aware QoS prediction approach. As a more reasonable and reliable source of the future values of dynamic QoS attributes, we believe that most QoS-based applications and approaches in services computing can benefit from QoS time series modeling and forecasting (if they need to know QoS information for future time periods to perform their working operations or processes). In addition, regarding this research concern, another possible research direction that has not been well-studied thus far is how to efficiently combine a prediction approach and its subsequent application; the combinations introduced in

Sect. 2 are intuitive and sensible, but more efficient integration may exist. Regarding the second reviewed concern, we exhaustively identify and categorize the different factors varied in the performed experiments of the reviewed studies. To provide comprehensive and rigorous evaluation and justification, each of the problem-based experimental configuration parameters should be independently varied, tested, and compared in an experiment. Finally, depending on the adopted approach and combined applications, each of their internal configuration settings (i.e., approach-specific and application-related settings) must also be identified and considered in experimentation.

Acknowledgement. This research is partially sponsored by the Ministry of Science and Technology (Taiwan) under the Grant MOST 108-2221-E-001-007-MY2.

References

1. Syu, Y., Wang, C.-M., Fanjiang, Y.-Y.: A survey of time-aware dynamic QOS forecasting research, its future challenges and research directions. In: Ferreira, J.E., Spanoudakis, G., Ma, Y., Zhang, L.-J. (eds.) SCC 2018. LNCS, vol. 10969, pp. 36–50. Springer, Cham (2018). https://doi.org/10.1007/978-3-319-94376-3_3
2. Syu, Y., Wang, C.-M.: QoS time series modeling and forecasting for web services: a comprehensive survey. IEEE Trans, Netw. Serv. Manage. (Under review)
3. Ding, S., Li, Y., Wu, D., Zhang, Y., Yang, S.: Time-aware cloud service recommendation using similarity-enhanced collaborative filtering and ARIMA model. Decis. Support Syst. **107**, 103–115 (2018). https://doi.org/10.1016/j.dss.2017.12.012
4. YunNi, X., Jian, D., Xin, L., QingSheng, Z.: Dependability prediction of WS-BPEL service compositions using petri net and time series models. In: 2013 IEEE 7th International Symposium on Service Oriented System Engineering (SOSE), Redwood City, pp. 192–202. IEEE (2013)
5. Li, M., Hua, Z., Zhao, J., Zou, Y., Xie, B.: ARIMA model-based web services trustworthiness evaluation and prediction. In: Liu, C., Ludwig, H., Toumani, F., Yu, Q. (eds.) ICSOC 2012. LNCS, vol. 7636, pp. 648–655. Springer, Heidelberg (2012). https://doi.org/10.1007/978-3-642-34321-6_51
6. Amin, A., Grunske, L., Colman, A.: An automated approach to forecasting QoS attributes based on linear and non-linear time series modeling. In: Proceedings of the 27th IEEE/ACM International Conference on Automated Software Engineering. Essen, Germany, pp. 130–139. ACM (2012). Sec. 2351695
7. Li, J., Zhao, Y., Ren, J., Ma, D.: Towards adaptive web services QoS prediction. In: 2010 IEEE International Conference on Service-Oriented Computing and Applications (SOCA), 13–15 December 2010, pp. 1–8 (2010). https://doi.org/10.1109/soca.2010.5707146
8. Fanjiang, Y.-Y., Syu, Y., Kuo, J.-Y.: Search based approach to forecasting QoS attributes of web services using genetic programming. Information and Software Technology, vol. 80, pp. 158–174 (2016). http://dx.doi.org/10.1016/j.infsof.2016.08.009
9. Syu, Y., Wang, C., Fanjiang, Y.: Modeling and forecasting of time-aware dynamic QoS attributes for cloud services. IEEE Trans. Netw. Serv. Manage. **16**, 1 (2018) https://doi.org/10.1109/tnsm.2018.2884983
10. Syu, Y., Kuo, J.-Y., Fanjiang, Y.-Y.: Time series forecasting for dynamic quality of web services: an empirical study. J. Syst. Softw. **134**, 279–303 (2017). https://doi.org/10.1016/j.jss.2017.09.011

11. Zhang, P., Wang, L., Li, W., Leung, H., Song, W.: A web service qos forecasting approach based on multivariate time series. In: 2017 IEEE International Conference on Web Services (ICWS), 25–30 June 2017, pp. 146–153 (2017). https://doi.org/10.1109/icws.2017.27

12. Ye, Z., Mistry, S., Bouguettaya, A., Dong, H.: Long-term QoS-aware cloud service composition using multivariate time series analysis. IEEE Trans. Serv. Comput. **9**(3), 382–393 (2016). https://doi.org/10.1109/TSC.2014.2373366

13. Nourikhah, H., Akbari, M.K., Kalantari, M.: Modeling and predicting measured response time of cloud-based web services using long-memory time series. J. Supercomput. **71**, 1–24 (2014). https://doi.org/10.1007/s11227-014-1317-4

14. Rahman, Z.U., Hussain, O.K., Hussain, F.K.: Time series QoS forecasting for management of cloud services. In: Proceedings of the 2014 Ninth International Conference on Broadband and Wireless Computing, Communication and Applications (2014)

15. Leitner, P., Ferner, J., Hummer, W., Dustdar, S.: Data-driven and automated prediction of service level agreement violations in service compositions. Distributed and Parallel Databases, journal article **31**(3), 447–470 (2013). https://doi.org/10.1007/s10619-013-7125-7

16. Amin, A., Colman, A., Grunske, L.: An approach to forecasting QoS attributes of web services based on ARIMA and GARCH models. In: 2012 IEEE 19th International Conference on Web Services (ICWS), Honolulu, HI, pp. 74–81. IEEE (2012)

17. Senivongse, T., Wongsawangpanich, N.: Composing services of different granularity and varying qos using genetic algorithm. In: Lecture Notes in Engineering and Computer Science: Proceedings of The World Congress on Engineering and Computer Science 2011, San Francisco, CA, USA, 19–21 October 2011, pp. 388-393 (2011)

18. Solomon, A., Litoiu, M.: Business process performance prediction on a tracked simulation model. In: Proceedings of the 3rd International Workshop on Principles of Engineering Service-Oriented Systems, Waikiki, Honolulu, HI, USA (2011)

19. Zadeh, M.H., Seyyedi, M.A.: Qos monitoring for web services by time series forecasting. In: 2010 3rd IEEE International Conference on Computer Science and Information Technology (ICCSIT), Chengdu, vol. 5. pp. 659–663. IEEE (2010)

20. Cavallo, B., Penta, M.D., Canfora, G.: An empirical comparison of methods to support QoS-aware service selection. In: Proceedings of the 2nd International Workshop on Principles of Engineering Service-Oriented Systems, Cape Town, South Africa, pp. 64–70. ACM (2010) sec. 1808899

21. Godse, M., Bellur, U., Sonar, R.: Automating QoS based service selection. In: 2010 IEEE International Conference on Web Services (ICWS), Miami, FL, pp. 534–541. IEEE (2010)

22. Mu, L., Jinpeng, H., Huipeng, G.: An adaptive web services selection method based on the QoS prediction mechanism. In: IEEE/WIC/ACM International Joint Conferences on Web Intelligence and Intelligent Agent Technologies, 2009. WI-IAT 2009, Milan, Italy, pp. 395–402. IET (2009)

23. Malak, J.S., Mohsenzadeh, M., Seyyedi, M.A.: Web service qos prediction based on multi agents. In: 2009 International Conference on Computer Technology and Development, 13–15 November 2009, vol. 1, pp. 265-269 (2009). https://doi.org/10.1109/icctd.2009.79

24. FanJiang, Y.-Y., Syu, Y.: Semantic-based automatic service composition with functional and non-functional requirements in design time: A genetic algorithm approach. Inf. Softw. Technol. **56**(3), 352–373 (2014). https://doi.org/10.1016/j.infsof.2013.12.001

25. Fanjiang, Y.-Y., Syu, Y., Ma, S.-P., Kuo, J.-Y.: An overview and classification of service description approaches in automated service composition research. IEEE Trans. Serv. Comput. **10**(2), 176–189 (2017)

26. Wagner, N., Michalewicz, Z., Khouja, M., McGregor, R.R.: Time series forecasting for dynamic environments: the DyFor genetic program model. IEEE Trans. Evol. Comput. **11**(4), 433–452 (2007). https://doi.org/10.1109/tevc.2006.882430

Web Service Composition by Optimizing Composition-Segment Candidates

Fang-Yuan Zuo, Ze-Han Shen, Shi-Liang Fan, and Yu-Bin Yang[✉]

State Key Laboratory for Novel Software Technology, Nanjing University,
Nanjing 210023, China
yangyubin@nju.edu.cn

Abstract. Web service composition has been increasingly challenging in recent years due to the escalating number of services and the diversity of task objectives. Despite many researches have already addressed the optimization of multiple Quality of Service (QoS) attributes, most of the currently available methods have to build a large web service dependency graph, which may incur excessive memory consumption and extreme inefficiency. To address these issues, we present a novel web service composition method by optimizing composition-segment candidates. Firstly, we formalize the web service composition problem as a Mixed-Integer Linear Programming (MILP) model and introduce some effective techniques for complex cases, and then a standard solver can be applied to this model. Afterwards, a candidate optimization method is proposed to solve the MILP model efficiently, which runs sharply fast without building a web service dependency graph. Experimental results on both Web Service Challenge 2009's datasets and substantial datasets randomly generated show that the proposed method outperforms the state-of-art while achieving a much ideal tradeoff among all the objectives with better performance.

Keywords: Web service composition · Optimization · MILP

1 Introduction

In service-oriented environments, many complex applications can be described as a series of processes invoking services selected at runtime. Thus, the web service composition problem has been widely studied [1,2]. Generally, many researchers aim at optimizing a single global QoS [3] by searching for a solution in a huge web service dependency graph [4]. When there are more than two objectives, i.e., QoS attributes considered, these methods usually fail to output a satisfactory solution. These QoS attributes are usually conflicted with each other, which makes it difficult to find a solution optimal for all the QoS attributes. Another shortcoming of these methods is that seeking a near-optimal solution in a huge dependency graph consumes much time and memory.

To address these issues, we aim at finding an ideal tradeoff among all the objectives without building a web service dependency graph. We formalize the

© Springer Nature Switzerland AG 2020
Q. Wang et al. (Eds.): SCC 2020, LNCS 12409, pp. 20–34, 2020.
https://doi.org/10.1007/978-3-030-59592-0_2

web service composition problem as a MILP model and apply a standard solver to it for a near-optimal solution. Furthermore, we present a candidate optimization method for a better tradeoff, which does not require any web service dependency graph. The main contributions of this paper are summarized as follows.

- We formalize the web service composition problem as a novel MILP model, which transforms min-max constraints into linear constraints by introducing integer variables.
- A standard solver is applied to the MILP model and outputs a near-optimal solution in most cases, and some effective techniques are introduced for complex cases.
- A candidate optimization method is proposed to solve the MILP model efficiently and obtains a composition with better tradeoff among all the objectives.

To validate the methods proposed in this paper, we carry out extensive experiments on both WSC-2009's datasets and randomly generated datasets.

The rest of this paper is organized as follows. Section 2 introduces the background and some related work. Section 3 formalizes the web service composition problem into a MILP model and provides some practically useful techniques. Section 4 proposes a candidate optimization method with no need to build a web service dependency graph. Section 5 presents the experimental results, and Sect. 6 provides the final remarks.

2   Background and Related Work

2.1   Background

The formal definition of web service is shown as follows.

Definition 1. *Giving a set of concepts C (the size of C is $|C| = m$), we define a Web Service ("service" for short) as a tuple $s_i = \{I_i, O_i, R_i, T_i\}$, where $I_i = \{i_1, \ldots, i_p\}$ is the subscript set of inputs required to invoke the web service s_i and $O_i = \{o_1, \ldots, o_q\}$ is the subscript set of outputs generated by invoking service s_i. Each element $c_j, j \in I_i \cup O_i$ is a semantic concept belonging to the set C, namely, $\{c_j | j \in I_i\} \subseteq C$ and $\{c_j | j \in O_i\} \subseteq C$. R_i and T_i are the nonfunctional attributes which are the measures for judging how well the service s_i serves the user.*

Obviously, services are not independent to each other. Relevant services can be combined by connecting matched inputs and outputs to construct compositions.

Lemma 1. *Giving an output c_o of a service s_i, as well as an input c_i of another service s_j, if c_o and c_i are equivalent concepts or c_o is a sub-concept of c_i, c_o matches c_i.*

Each service has its own QoS, which contributes to the global QoS of a composition. The definition of QoS of a web service composition is dependent on the structure of composition. There are two main kinds of structures, named *sequential structure* and *parallel structure*. The first one means the services are invoked in order, while the second one means they are invoked synchronously.

Definition 2. *A composition containing the set of services $S = \{s_1, \ldots, s_n\}$ is defined as Ω. If the services are chained in sequence, the composition is expressed as $\Omega^{\rightarrow} = s_1 \rightarrow \ldots \rightarrow s_n$; if in parallel, it is expressed as $\Omega^{\|} = s_1 \| \ldots \| s_n$. The set of services involved in Ω is defined as $Servs(\Omega) = S$. Moreover, the length of a composition Ω is defined as $Len(\Omega) = |S|$, namely, the number of services in Ω. Taking the response time as an example, we compute the global QoS of Ω as follow.*

$$\left.\begin{array}{l} RT(\Omega^{\rightarrow}) = \sum_{i=1}^{n} RT(s_i), s_i \in S \\ RT(\Omega^{\|}) = \max_{1 \leq i \leq n} RT(s_i), s_i \in S \end{array}\right\} \tag{1}$$

where $RT(\Omega)$ represents the global response time of the composition and $RT(s)$ represents the same of services s. Another QoS attribute is throughput, which can be defined as follows:

$$\left.\begin{array}{l} TP(\Omega^{\rightarrow}) = \min_{1 \leq i \leq n} TP(s_i), s_i \in S \\ TP(\Omega^{\|}) = \min_{1 \leq i \leq n} TP(s_i), s_i \in S \end{array}\right\} \tag{2}$$

where $TP(\Omega)$ and $TP(s)$ represent the global throughput and the service throughput similarly.

Based on the above concepts, Multi-Objective Web Service Composition can be described as Definition 3.

Definition 3. *Giving a web services set S, a concepts set C and a given composition request $R = \{In_R, Out_R\}$, we define Multi-Objective Web Service Composition as finding a composition Ω which archives an ideal tradeoff among $Len(\Omega), RT(\Omega)$ and $TP(\Omega)$.*

2.2   Related Work

In this subsection, we introduce some related works about single objective and multi-objective web service composition. Meanwhile, we point out their main drawbacks at last.

2.2.1   Single Objective Web Service Composition

For the single objective web service composition, the most popular objective is the number of services in the final composition.

A heuristic A^* search algorithm was proposed in [5] for web service composition, which used A^* search algorithm in a dependency graph. Noting that some useless services might exist in the final composition, Xia et al. [6] proposed an algorithm to remove the useless service, which was useful to reduce the number of services. Fan et al. [4] transformed the web service composition problem into a dynamic knapsack problem and applied dynamic programming technique on it, which obtained a solution containing a small number of services.

Single objectives web service composition fails to meet the requirements in many applications. Therefore, many researchers pay more attention to multi-objective service composition of which goal is to find a proper composition achieving an ideal tradeoff among all the objectives.

2.2.2 Multi-objective Web Service Composition

Graphs are natural and intuitive ways to express the complex interaction relations between entities. The web service dependency graph is useful to illustrate the multi-objective web service composition problem. In Fig. 1, a web service composition problem is shown as a layered directed graph. The composition request is $R = \{\{in_1, in_2, in_3\}, \{out_1, out_2, out_3, out_4\}\}$. Each rectangle in the graph represents a web service. The response time and throughput of a web service are shown in the above and below, respectively. Each circle represents an input or an output of a service. In addition, the edges connecting circles and rectangles denote the matching relations between them. Two dummy service S_i for the inputs and S_o for the outputs are added in the graph, whose response time and throughputs are 0 ms and $+\infty$ inv/s respectively.

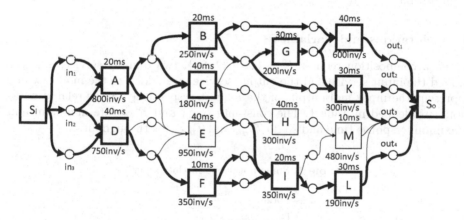

Fig. 1. An example of a service dependency graph.

As shown in the Fig. 1, there are many compositions with different QoS and numbers of services satisfying the request R. The composition highlighted in the graph $\Omega = S_0 \to (A||D) \to (B||C||F) \to (G||I) \to (J||K||L) \to S_o$ is the optimal with response time of 110 ms. In addition, the throughput of Ω is 180 inv/s, which is not optimal. Moreover, another composition $\Omega' = S_i \to (A||D) \to (B||E||F) \to (G||I) \to (J||K||L) \to S_o$, has a response time of 130 ms, a throughput of 190 inv/s and the same length of 12. On the one hand, the response time of Ω is shorter in comparison with the one of Ω'. On the another hand, the throughput of Ω is less than Ω'. Although both Ω and Ω' are Pareto optimal solutions, we prefer the former since $TP(\Omega')$ changes little from $TP(\Omega)$ (180 inv/s to 190 inv/s), while the response time of Ω has been greatly improved (130 ms versus 110 ms).

To deal with the above problems, Zeng et al. [7] directly transformed the multi-objective service composition into single-objective optimization and used traditional techniques to solve it. Furthermore, some researchers applied a systematic search algorithm like Dijkstra's algorithm with the same single-objective function [8], which generated many solutions and recorded the best one until no more concepts could be generated. Another important objective is the number of services in the resulting composition, which is necessary to consider for conducting services composition. Fan et al. [9] used a Knapsack-Variant algorithm with transforming multi-objectives into one loss objective computed dynamically. However, these methods have to build a huge dependency graph explicitly, which leads to a long composition time, especially in an enormous number of services situation.

3   MILP Formalization of Web Service Composition

In this section, the problem of web service composition is formalized as a MILP model. Once a MILP model of web service composition is obtained, some standard solvers such as groubi [10], can be applied to it and output a well enough composition.

3.1   Notations and Variables

Given a composition request $R = \{In_R, Out_R\}$, two dummy services s_0, s_{n+1} named the input service and the output service, are added to the model, which represent the input and output of the request respectively. Some related notations are defined in Table 1. The constants R_{min} and R_{max} are minimum and maximum response time and so do T_{min} and T_{max} for throughput.

Table 1. Some notations in this paper

Name	Notation	Description
Service set	S	$S = \{s_0, \ldots, s_{n+1}\}$
Concept set	C	$C = \{c_1, \ldots, c_m\}$
Service input	I_i	The input set of s_i is $\{c_j \mid j \in I_i\}$, $I_0 = \varnothing, I_{n+1} = Out_R$
Service output	O_i	The output set of s_i is $\{c_j \mid j \in O_i\}$, $O_0 = In_R, O_{n+1} = \varnothing$
Response time	R_i	The response time of s_i and $R_0 = R_{n+1} = R_{min}$
Throughput	T_i	The throughput of s_i, $T_0 = T_{n+1} = T_{max}$ specially

For a formal description, we introduce some variables optimized by standard solver in Table 2. In the composition context of this paper, the term *response time* is treated as *generated time* of a concept or *invoked time* of a service.

Table 2. The variables in MILP model

Notation	Range	Description
x_i	$\{0,1\}$	$x_i = 1$ means s_i is selected
y_j	$\{0,1\}$	$y_j = 1$ means c_i is generated
sr_i	$[0,+\infty)$	The time when s_i has been invoked
r_j	$[0,+\infty)$	The time when c_j is generated at first time
st_i	$[0,+\infty)$	The throughput of s_i in the composition
t_j	$[0,+\infty)$	The throughput of c_j in the composition

3.2   Criteria

Taking response time, throughput, and number of services into consideration, we can formalize the criteria of this MILP model as follows:

$$\max_{x,y,sr,r,st,t} st_{n+1} - \alpha \sum_{i=1}^{n} x_i - \beta sr_{n+1} \tag{3}$$

where α and β are weights of different single objectives, and they can be assigned flexibly to adapt to the preference of user.

3.3   Constraints

Without building a huge dependency graph, we add some constraints to the proposed MILP model, which guarantees that a solution of the MILP model is also a valid web service composition.

3.3.1   Input and Output Constraints

For the input and output services, they must be invoked:

$$x_0 = x_{n+1} = 1 \tag{4}$$

One service can be invoked until its whole input concepts have been generated. A concept cannot be generated unless at least one service whose output set contains it has been invoked.

$$|I_i|x_i \leq \sum_{j \in I_i} y_j, \ i = 0,\ldots,n+1 \tag{5}$$

$$y_j \leq \sum_{i \in \{k|j \in O_k\}} x_i, \ j = 1,\ldots,m \tag{6}$$

If sets I_i in (5) and $\{k|j \in O_k\}$ in (6) are empty sets, the right sides of them are treated as zero.

3.3.2 Response Time Constraints

In the MILP model, we pay attention to the criteria consisting of three parts. The first part of criteria is to minimize the invoked time sr_{n+1} of output service s_{n+1}, so only the lower bound need to be given. For each service, the constraint of response time is shown as follows:

$$\left.\begin{array}{l} sr_i \geq (1 - x_i)R_{max} \\ sr_i \geq R_i \\ sr_i \geq R_i + r_j, j \in I_i \end{array}\right\} \quad i = 0, 1, \ldots, n+1 \tag{7}$$

The first inequality in (7) makes the invoked time sr_i reach the maximum response time $R_{\max}$ while s_i is not selected. The third inequality makes the response time sr_i satisfy the definition of response time in Definition 2 when s_i is selected. A special case is that the set I_i is an empty set, such as I_0, in which the third equation makes no sense (no constraint). To handle this case correctly, we introduce the second inequality in which sr_i is greater than or equal to its original response time R_i. For example, the response time sr_0 of input service s_0 equals to R_0.

The generated time constraints of each concept are defined as follows.

$$r_j = \begin{cases} R_{\max} & \text{if } \{k|j \in O_k\} = \varnothing \\ \min_{i \in \{k|j \in O_k\}} sr_i & \text{otherwise} \end{cases} \quad j = 1, \ldots, m \tag{8}$$

However, it's esoteric that the minimum part in (8) can be transformed into a linear constraint [11]. We introduce variables $l_{ji} \in [0, +\infty), z_{ji} \in \{0,1\}$ for each $r_j, i \in \{k|j \in O_k\}$, which ensure the equivalence between the minimum part of (8) and (9).

$$\left.\begin{array}{ll} r_j & \leq sr_i, & \forall i \in \{k|j \in O_k\} \\ r_j & \geq sr_i - l_{ji}, & \forall i \in \{k|j \in O_k\} \\ l_i & \leq (1 - z_{ji})R_{max}, & \forall i \in \{k|j \in O_k\} \\ \sum_{i \in \{k|j \in O_k\}} z_{ji} = 1 \end{array}\right\}, \quad j = 1, 2, \ldots, m \tag{9}$$

3.3.3 Throughput Constraints

Similarly, we only need to give an upper bound for throughput, since the criteria focus on the maximum throughput of output service. The throughput of a service depends on the throughputs of its input concepts and its own throughput, more precisely, on the minimum of them. If one service is not selected, we let its throughput to be T_{min} reasonably.

$$\left.\begin{array}{l} st_i \leq T_i x_i + (1 - x_i)T_{min} \\ st_i \leq t_j, \forall j \in I_i \end{array}\right\}, \quad i = 0, 1, \ldots, n+1 \tag{10}$$

Intuitively, the throughput of a concept is the maximum throughputs of all services which can generate the concept.

$$t_j = \begin{cases} T_{\min} & \text{if } \{k|j \in O_k\} = \varnothing \\ \max_{\forall i \in \{k|j \in O_k\}} st_i & \text{otherwise} \end{cases} \quad j = 1, \ldots, m \tag{11}$$

As same as the constraints of service generated time, the maximum part in (11) can be transformed into a linear constraint by introducing variables $g_{ji} \in [0, +\infty), u_{ji} \in \{0, 1\}$.

$$\left. \begin{array}{rll} t_j & \geq st_i, & \forall i \in \{k|j \in O_k\} \\ t_j & \leq sr_i + g_{ji}, & \forall i \in \{k|j \in O_k\} \\ g_i & \leq (1 - u_{ji})T_{max}, & \forall i \in \{k|j \in O_k\} \\ \sum_{i \in \{k|j \in O_k\}} u_{ji} = 1 & & \end{array} \right\}, \quad j = 1, \ldots, m \quad (12)$$

3.4 Practical Techniques for MILP Model

QoS-aware web service composition can be seen as an NP-hard problem, for which there are no effective algorithms [12]. In practical terms, the above MILP model equivalent to the original problem works not well in some cases. For this reason, some effective techniques are applied to improve the performance of the MILP model.

3.4.1 Throughput Constraints Simplification

The vital part of (3) is the throughput of output service, while the throughputs of other services are inconsequential. We notice that the throughput of output service in a composition is the minimum throughput of all the selected services. Consequently, we can obtain the final correct throughput of output service with the following steps.

- Let the throughputs of selected services (expect s_{n+1}) to be their original throughputs.
- Let other throughputs to be T_{max}.
- Take the minimum throughput of all services as the throughput of output service.

The formalized description (13) can replace (10), (11) and (12), which reduces many constraints and variables. The second minimum equation can be transformed into linear constraints with the similar method used in (9).

$$\left. \begin{array}{l} st_i = T_i x_i + (1 - x_i)T_{max}, i = 0, 1, \ldots, n \\ st_{n+1} = \min_{i=0}^{n} st_i \end{array} \right\} \quad (13)$$

3.4.2 Response Time Constraints Approximation

However, there are numerous integer variables introduced in the response time constraints, which causes a serious performance problem while applying a standard solver.

$$\left. \begin{array}{l} sr_i = R_i x_i + (1 - x_i)R_{max}, i = 0, 1, \ldots, n \\ sr_{n+1} = \sum_{i=0}^{n} sr_i \end{array} \right\} \quad (14)$$

An efficient method is to replace the response time of output service with the sum of the response time of all chosen services, and the detail is described in (14). It does greatly shorten the execution time while holding well enough criteria, even though the approximations of response time constraints are not completely accurate.

In summary, the MILP model with these techniques can be solved efficiently without building a huge and complex dependency graph. Extensive experiments applying groubi [10] solver are presented in Sect. 5. We notice that there is an obvious gap between the MILP method and other methods, which means we can still make great progress. Therefore, we propose a more effective and efficient mechanism in the next section.

4   Composition-Segment Candidate Optimization

In this section, a mechanism of optimizing composition-segments candidates is proposed to improve the performance of the MILP model. We define four kinds of segment candidates in Definition 4, and the core idea of this mechanism is to improve the score segment candidate in current composition with three other kinds of segment candidates.

Definition 4. *Composition-Segment Candidate ("segment candidate" for short) of a service is defined as a local composition whose last service is exactly the service. For a concept, its composition-segment candidate can generate it. Similar to the criteria (3) of MILP model, the score of a composition-segment Ω_s is defined as:*

$$Score(\Omega_s) = TP(\Omega_s) - \alpha * Len(\Omega_s) - \beta * RT(\Omega_s) \qquad (15)$$

For each service and concept, we maintain four kinds of segment candidates— S_s, N_s, R_s and T_s, which hold the best current segment candidates of different objectives—score, length, response time and throughput respectively.

4.1   Generating Composition-Segment Candidates

To generate segment candidates, we construct the current output map M_c firstly, of which the keys are services or concepts and the values are lists of segment candidates.

Table 3. Segment candidates related to service I with $\alpha = 100, \beta = 20$

Candidate no	Composition-segment	Len	RT (ms)	TP (inv/s)	Score
1	$S_i \to A \to C$	3	60	180	−1320
2	$S_i \to A\|\|D \to E$	4	80	750	−1250
3	$S_i \to D \to F$	3	50	350	−950
4	$S_i \to A\|\|D \to C\|\|F \to I$	6	80	180	−2020
5	$S_i \to A\|\|D \to E\|\|F \to I$	6	100	350	−2250

Algorithm 1 takes service s_i and map M_c as inputs and checks whether service s_i can be invoked at line 2. Then, it initializes the list P_s with four sets of precursors and adds all precursors to these sets respectively. The following step is to create four candidates in order and assign their precursor sets with P_s respectively. Finally, the method *update_attribute* calculates their score, length and QoS, and we append the four candidates to list P_c.

Algorithm 1: Generating Composition-Segment Candidates

Input: s_i, M_c
Output: P_c
1 $P_c \leftarrow []$
2 **if** $I_i \subseteq M_c.keys$ **then**
3 | $P_s \leftarrow [set(), set(), set(), set()]$
4 | **for** concept $c \in I_i$ **do**
5 | **for** segment $i, s \in M_c[c]$ **do**
6 | $P_s[i].add(s)$
7 | **for** segments set $p_s \in P_s$ **do**
8 | $s \leftarrow$ SegmentCandidate(s_i)
9 | $s.pre \leftarrow p_s$
10 | update_attribute(s)
11 | $P_c.append(s)$
12 **return** P_c

Taking the generating process of service I in Fig. 1 as an example, we list some segment candidates related with service I in Table 3 and shows the detailed process in Fig. 2. Service I has three input concepts i_1, i_2, i_3, and their segment candidates are listed in the left (the green cell denotes score segment candidate). For each kind of segment candidate, the newly generated candidate combines the corresponding candidates of its inputs respectively. For example, the score segment candidate (Candidate 5 in Table 3) of I consists of Candidate 2—the score segment candidate of i_1, and Candidate 3—the score segment candidate of i_2 and i_3.

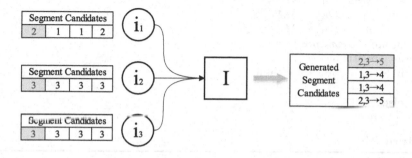

Fig. 2. Segment candidates generation

4.2   Optimizing Composition-Segment Candidates

After generating the segment candidates, the next step is to optimize the score segment candidate with other kinds of segment candidates. We firstly analyze the bottlenecks of score segment candidate. Algorithm 2 shows the process of analyzing bottlenecks of score segment candidate S_s.

Algorithm 2: Analyzing Bottlenecks of Candidate

    Input: S_s
    Output: L_b

1 $L_b \leftarrow [null, null, null]$
2 $B_l \leftarrow 0, B_r \leftarrow R_{min}, B_t \leftarrow T_{max}$
3 **for** segment $s \in S_s.$pre **do**
4   **if** $Len(s) > B_l$ **then**
5        $B_l = \text{Len}(s), L_b[0] = s.$concept
6   **if** $RT(s) > B_r$ **then**
7        $B_r = \text{RT}(s), L_b[1] = s.$concept
8   **if** $TP(s) < B_t$ **then**
9        $B_t = \text{TP}(s), L_b[2] = s.$concept

10 **return** L_b

For a score segment candidate S_s, Algorithm 2 finds its three kinds of bottlenecks. The operations from line 4 to 6 find the precursor with maximum length and record the corresponding concept in L_b. Similar operations are performed with response time bottleneck. On the contrary, the throughput bottleneck gets the minimal throughput concept of them.

Algorithm 3: Improving Bottlenecks of Candidate

    Input: M_c, P_c
    Output: P_c

1 **while** *True* **do**
2     $S_s \leftarrow P_c[0], S'_s \leftarrow S_s, L_b \leftarrow bottleneck\_analyze(S'_s)$
3     $score\_pre\_set \leftarrow S'_s.$pre, $b_1, b_2, b_3 = L_b$
4     $score\_pre\_set[b_1] \leftarrow M_c[b_1][1]$
5     $score\_pre\_set[b_2] \leftarrow M_c[b_2][2]$
6     $score\_pre\_set[b_3] \leftarrow M_c[b_2][3]$
7     $S'_s.$pre $\leftarrow score\_pre\_set$
8     $update\_attribute(S'_s)$
9   **if** $S'_s.score > S_s.score$ **then**
10       $P_c[0] \leftarrow S'_s$
11   **else**
12   break

13 **return** P_c

Algorithm 3 improves the score segment candidate S_s in list P_c. Taking current output map M_c and candidates list P_c as the inputs, we use Algorithm 2 to get bottlenecks L_b, and then replace bottleneck candidates with the currently best candidates in M_c to improve S_s. Finally, the near-optimal score segment candidate S_s is generated by repeating the two foregoing steps until the score of S_s isn't able to be greater.

As shown in Fig. 2, the optimal score segment candidate is Candidate 4 instead of Candidate 5 (whose color is red). By calling Algorithm 2, we can obtain bottlenecks $L_b = [i_1, i_1, i_2]$. Then, Algorithm 3 handles each bottleneck of L_b in a same way. Taking the first element i_1 in L_b as an example, we replace the score segment candidate(Candidate 2) of i_1 with its length segment candidate(Candidate 1) in S_s, which reduce its length. Finally, the score segment candidate of I becomes Candidate 4.

4.3   Greedy Selection

Having generated four candidates P_c of service s_i and optimized the score candidate S_s in P_c, we compare each kind of candidate in P_c with the corresponding one in previous list $M_c[s_i]$ respectively and store the better ones. If the map M_c does not contain s_i, we insert the key-value pair (s_i, P_c) into M_c directly. For each output concept of s_i, we create four kinds of segment candidates and assign their precursors with the corresponding service candidates in P_c. Then, we perform similar operations to reserve the better ones. After greedy selection, Candidate 4 is reserved as the final score segment candidate of service I in Fig. 2.

By repeating the three above steps until the output map M_c is not changing, the score segment candidate of output service s_{n+1} appears, and the final composition is achieved.

5   Experimental Results

Extensive experiments have been carried out to evaluate the performance of our proposed methods. To make the conclusion more convincing, we evaluate our methods on two different groups of datasets.

Table 4. The characteristics of datasets

Datasets	D-01	D-02	D-03	D-04	D-05	R-01	R-02	R-03	R-04	R-05
#Service	572	4129	8138	8301	15211	1000	3000	5000	7000	9000
RT.opt (ms)	500	1690	760	1470	4070	1430	975	805	1225	1420
TP.opt (inv/s)	15000	6000	4000	4000	4000	1000	2500	1500	2000	2500
Len.opt	5	20	10	40	30	7	12	12	14	16

5.1   Datasets

To evaluate the performance of the proposed composition mechanisms, we conducted a group of experiments using five public repositories from the Web Service Challenge 2009 and five randomly generated datasets. As shown in Table 4, the group of datasets of the WSC 2009 ranges from 572 to 15211 services. We evaluate further the performance of our algorithms with another group of datasets[1]. And the optimal values (RT.opt, TP.opt, Len.opt) of single objectives for each dataset are shown in it, which are computed by the memory-based algorithm.

5.2   Performance Analysis

To validate our approaches, we compare them with three different the-state-of-arts in the same experimental environment. For each dataset, we mainly show the solicitude for the global QoS of generated solution (RT for response time and TP for throughput), the length of composition (Len) and the execution time of method ($Time$ including the time of building service dependency graphs).

Table 5. Detailed comparisons with other methods

Datasets		D-01	D-02	D-03	D-04	D-05	R-01	R-02	R-03	R-04	R-05
Method in [13]	RT (ms)	500	1690	760	1470	4070	1430	975	805	1225	1420
	TP (inv/s)	3000	3000	2000	2000	1000	1000	1000	500	1000	500
	Len	10	20	10	42	33	8	19	18	21	19
	Time (ms)	73	1324	3591	10121	14925	26	161	531	1023	2066
	RT (ms)	840	2200	2450	4150	4990	1430	1305	1520	2095	1975
	TP (inv/s)	15000	6000	4000	2000	4000	1000	2500	1500	2000	2500
	Len	5	20	10	44	32	13	18	20	30	19
	Time (ms)	68	1373	3736	9283	12717	38	175	503	992	2053
Method in [14]	RT (ms)	760	2270	1300	2140	5340	1580	1815	1640	1840	2300
	TP (inv/s)	10000	6000	3000	1000	4000	1000	2000	1000	2000	1500
	Len	6	21	12	47	36	9	18	17	19	20
	Time (ms)	70	1252	3795	9813	14544	25	163	473	845	2096
Method in [9]	RT (ms)	680	1800	760	1600	4260	1430	975	1090	1225	1605
	TP (inv/s)	14000	6000	4000	3500	4000	1000	2000	1500	2000	2500
	Len	5	20	10	43	33	8	16	15	17	18
	Time (ms)	317	1684	3713	10651	13223	76	443	1136	1804	1613
MILP Method ($\alpha = 1, \beta = 0.2$)	RT (ms)	760	2050	810	3560	4130	1430	1560	1535	1620	2210
	TP (inv/s)	15000	6000	4000	4000	4000	1000	2500	1500	2000	2500
	Len	5	20	10	62	30	7	12	12	15	16
	Time (ms)	196	1113	2138	3558	4723	245	964	2259	3058	4828
Candidate Optimization Method ($\alpha = 10, \beta = 7$)	RT (ms)	680	1800	790	1470	4260	1430	975	805	1225	1420
	TP (inv/s)	15000	6000	4000	2000	4000	1000	2000	500	2000	2500
	Len	6	23	12	45	41	8	16	16	15	18
	Time (ms)	**35**	**98**	**72**	**459**	**274**	**7**	**75**	**90**	**101**	**230**

As shown in Table 5, [13] can generate two different solutions (one with the optimal response time and another with the optimal throughput). The method in [9] makes an excellent tradeoff of three attributes. Obviously, the execution time of compositions generated by methods [13], [14] and [9] is so long that some of them are longer than ten seconds. Moreover, our candidate optimization method runs not only fast but also archives ideal tradeoffs.

---

[1] https://wiki.citius.usc.es/inv:downloadable_results:ws-random-qos.

To measure the performance intuitively, we define $Ability(RT) = \frac{RT.opt}{RT}$, $Ability(TP) = \frac{TP}{TP.opt}$, $Ability(Len) = \frac{Len.opt}{Len}$ and $Ability(Time) = \frac{min(Time)}{Time}$. Moreover, we have $Ability(RT, TP) = [Ability(RT) + Ability(TP)]/2$, and the whole performance $Ability(RT, TP, Len, Time)$ is defined in the same manner. As shown in Fig. 3, the candidate optimization method has an outstanding $Ability(Time)$ and outperforms other methods in $Ability(RT, TP, Len, Time)$.

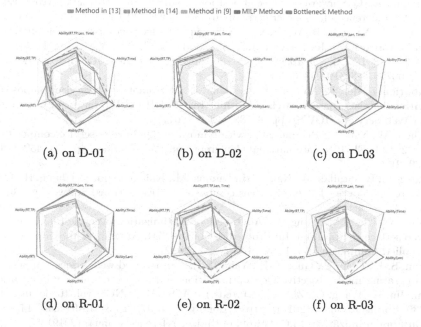

Fig. 3. Radar charts to compare the performance of five methods on several datasets.

6   Conclusions

In this paper, we formalize the multi-objective web service composition problem as a MILP model and propose a candidate optimization method to solve the model effectively and efficiently. A large number of experiments show that our candidate optimization method runs sharply fast while performing better than the state-of-the-art on QoS and number of services. Both the MILP method and the candidate optimization method save much running time with no need to build a service dependency graph.

Acknowledgment. This work is funded by the National Natural Science Foundation of China (No. 61673204), and the Fundamental Research Funds for the Central Universities (No. 14380046).

References

1. Jiang, W., Zhang, C., Huang, Z., Chen, M., Hu, S., Liu, Z.: Qsynth: a tool for QoS-aware automatic service composition. In: 2010 IEEE International Conference on Web Services, pp. 42–49. IEEE (2010)
2. Wagner, F., Ishikawa, F., Honiden, S.: QoS-aware automatic service composition by applying functional clustering. In: 2011 IEEE International Conference on Web Services, pp. 89–96. IEEE (2011)
3. Strunk, A.: QoS-aware service composition: a survey. In: 2010 Eighth IEEE European Conference on Web Services, pp. 67–74. IEEE (2010)
4. Fan, S.-L., Yang, Y.-B., Wang, X.-X.: Efficient web service composition via knapsack-variant algorithm. In: Ferreira, J.E., Spanoudakis, G., Ma, Y., Zhang, L.-J. (eds.) SCC 2018. LNCS, vol. 10969, pp. 51–66. Springer, Cham (2018). https://doi.org/10.1007/978-3-319-94376-3_4
5. Rodriguez-Mier, P., Mucientes, M., Lama, M.: Automatic web service composition with a heuristic-based search algorithm. In: 2011 IEEE International Conference on Web Services (ICWS), pp. 81–88. IEEE (2011)
6. Chen, M., Yan, Y.: Redundant service removal in QoS-aware service composition. In: 2012 IEEE 19th International Conference on Web Services, pp. 431–439. IEEE (2012)
7. Zeng, L., Benatallah, B., Ngu, A.H., Dumas, M., Kalagnanam, J., Chang, H.: QoS-aware middleware for web services composition. IEEE Trans. Softw. Eng. **30**(5), 311–327 (2004)
8. Yan, Y., Chen, M., Yang, Y.: Anytime QoS optimization over the PlanGraph for web service composition. In: Proceedings of the 27th Annual ACM Symposium on Applied Computing, pp. 1968–1975. ACM (2012)
9. Fan, S.-L., Ding, F., Guo, C.-H., Yang, Y.-B.: Supervised web service composition integrating multi-objective QoS optimization and service quantity minimization. In: Jin, H., Wang, Q., Zhang, L.-J. (eds.) ICWS 2018. LNCS, vol. 10966, pp. 215–230. Springer, Cham (2018). https://doi.org/10.1007/978-3-319-94289-6_14
10. Gurobi Optimization, LLC: Gurobi optimizer reference manual (2019)
11. Bertsimas, D., Mazumder, R., et al.: Least quantile regression via modern optimization. Ann. Stat. **42**(6), 2494–2525 (2014)
12. Jatoth, C., Gangadharan, G., Buyya, R.: Computational intelligence based QoS-aware web service composition: a systematic literature review. IEEE Trans. Serv. Comput. **10**(3), 475–492 (2015)
13. Xia, Y.M., Yang, Y.B.: Web service composition integrating QoS optimization and redundancy removal. In: 2013 IEEE 20th International Conference on Web Services, pp. 203–210. IEEE (2013)
14. Chattopadhyay, S., Banerjee, A., Banerjee, N.: A scalable and approximate mechanism for web service composition. In: 2015 IEEE International Conference on Web Services (ICWS), pp. 9–16. IEEE (2015)

Collaborative Learning Using LSTM-RNN for Personalized Recommendation

Benjamin A. Kwapong$^{(\boxtimes)}$, Richard Anarfi, and Kenneth K. Fletcher

University of Massachusetts Boston, Boston, MA 02125, USA
{benjamin.kwapong001,richard.anarfi001,kenneth.fletcher}@umb.edu

Abstract. Today, the ability to track users' sequence of online activities, makes identifying their evolving preferences for recommendation practicable. However, despite the myriad of available online activity information, most existing time-based recommender systems either focus on predicting some user rating, or rely on information from similar users. These systems, therefore, disregard the temporal and contextual aspects of users preferences, revealed in the rich and useful historical sequential information, which can potentially increase recommendation accuracy. In this work, we consider such rich, user online activity sequence, as a complex dependency of each user's consumption sequence, and combine the concept of collaborative filtering with long short-term memory recurrent neural network (LSTM-RNN), to make personalized recommendations. Specifically, we use encoder-decoder LSTM-RNN, to make sequence-to-sequence recommendations. Our proposed model builds on the strength of collaborative filtering while preserving individual user preferences for personalized recommendation. We conduct experiments using Movielens (https://grouplens.org/datasets/movielens) dataset to evaluate our proposed model and empirically demonstrate that it improves recommendation accuracy when compared to state-of-the-art recommender systems.

Keywords: Recommender systems · Deep learning · Neural networks · Recurrent neural networks · Long short-term memory RNN · Sequence-to-sequence recommendations

1 Introduction

The comfort, simplicity and extensive reach of the internet has altered the traditional approach to marketing and commerce leading to a dominant new brand, e-commerce and marketing. In this new form of service provision and commerce approach, users become overwhelmed by abundance and variety of products and services, resulting in the challenge of choice making. To ease this challenge the use of recommender systems (RS) has recently become a subject of interest.

RS are one of the most successful applications of data mining and machine learning technology in practice. They are typically based on the matrix completion problem formulation, where for each user-item-pair only one interaction (e.g., a rating) is considered [1]. Collaborative filtering (CF) is one of such

Q. Wang et al. (Eds.): SCC 2020, LNCS 12409, pp. 35–49, 2020.
https://doi.org/10.1007/978-3-030-59592-0_3

widely used and more effective service recommendation techniques. It bases its recommendations on the ratings or behavior of other users in the system [2,3]. Traditional memory- and model-based CF recommendation methods, although useful, are far from perfect, due to their disregard of time. Thus, they assume consumption events to be independent from each other, which precludes such methods from taking advantage of the temporal dynamics that naturally exist in user behavior, for personalized recommendation. This makes them unsuitable to capture the temporal aspects of recommendations, such as user evolving preferences or taste or context-dependent interests [4]. This is because, there are many application scenarios where considering short-term user interests and longer-term sequential patterns can be central to the success of a recommender system [1]. For instance, to predict the next best item from a user sequential events, sequential logs can also be used to derive longer-term behavior patterns, to detect interest drifts of individual users over time, identify short-term popularity trends in the community that can be exploited by recommendation algorithms, or to reason about the best point in time to remind users of certain items they have seen or purchased before [1].

Modern recurrent neural networks (RNN), such as the long short-term memory (LSTM), have proven very capable for sequence prediction problems and are well-suited to capture the evolution of users taste [5]. As a result, Devooght and Bersini [4] showed that CF can be viewed as a sequence prediction and demonstrated that by applying LSTM-RNN to CF recommendations. Their work however, does not consider user sequential event information and so fails to personalize recommendations. Similar to our proposed method is the works proposed by Ko et al. [6] and Donkers et al. [7]. In their work, Ko et al. [6] proposed a collaborative RNN for dynamic recommender systems. They studied sequential form of user event data and, by using ideas from CF, proposed a collaborative sequence model based on RNN. Also, Donkers et al. [7] proposed a sequential user-based RNN recommendation method. They showed, in their work, how individual users can be represented in addition to sequences of consumed items in a Gated Recurrent Unit (GRU), to effectively produce personalized next item recommendations.

These works, however, have some limitations. First, they are not powerful enough to represent and capture the complex dependencies that may exist within user event sequences, especially, when the sequences are very long and might be of variable lengths. Second, they fail to generate a distributed representation (embedding) of the input sequence, which reduces the task performance of their proposed models. Third, they base their recommendation on predicting either the next item in the sequence or a fixed number of items in a sequence and that makes them impractical, especially for applications where recommending items in variable sequence length sequence is expected.

To address the above limitations, this paper employs Encoder-Decoder LSTM-RNN, which is suitable for processing user sequence event data, for sequence-to-sequence recommendations. We build a flexible model to represent complex dependencies within long sequences, by building a stronger correlation between user consumption sequence. We achieve this by modeling each user consumption instance as a dependency on all previous consumptions for personalize recommendations. The summary of our contributions are as follows:

1. We build a strong correlation between user consumption sequence by modeling each user's consumption instance as a dependency on all previous consumptions. This allows us the ability to represent complex dependencies within long sequences and explore the extra details and information embedded in sequential events in order to preserve user preferences.
2. We employ encoder-decoder LSTM-RNN because of the length of consumption preferences of users. LSTM-RNNs work better on long-term dependencies than traditional RNNs.
3. We build on the strength of collaborative filtering, by using other user's consumption preferences, while preserving individual user preferences and improves personalize recommendation accuracy. This bridges the gap created by most existing models, where recommendation is based on either modeling each user's individual preferences or describing all users by a single prototypical behavioral profile (global learning).
4. We perform experiments to evaluate our proposed model and compare it to baseline methods such as Bayesian Personalized Ranking Matrix Factorization [8] and Adaptive Hinge Pairwise Matrix Factorization [9].

The remainder of this paper is as follows. In Sect. 2 we discuss works related to sequence-to-sequence recommendations, then RNN-based CF recommendation methods and finally, personalized recommendations using RNN. Our proposed work is discussed in detail in Sect. 3. In Sect. 4, we present experiments to evaluate our proposed method and also discuss our results. Finally, the paper is concluded in Sect. 5.

2   Related Works

This section reviews several existing works in literature related to our proposed work. We also provide a distinction between our proposed method and existing related works.

2.1   Sequence-to-Sequence (seq2seq) Recommender Systems

Many real world problems can be modeled as sequence-to-sequence (seq2seq) problems [10–12]. Recurrent neural networks (RNNs) have proven to be an effective tool in seq2seq predictions. This has led to some very useful work in the area of seq2seq predictions using RNN techniques. Chu et al. [13] built a RNN for seq2seq prediction using GRU. The network treats a user's recent ratings or behaviors as an ordered sequence. Each of these user ratings or behaviors is modeled by the network's hidden layers. Furthermore, they integrate the GRU with back propagation neural network to increase the prediction accuracy. Hidasi et al. [14] proposed a session-based recommendation method by modifying the basic GRU-RNN. The GRU-RNN modification was achieved by introducing session-parallel mini-batches based output sampling and ranking loss function. In their work, the network input is the actual state of the session while the output is the item of the next event in the session. For stability purposes, the input vector was normalized and this reinforced their memory effect.

In their work, Kuan et al. [15] proposed a Heterogeneous Attribute Recurrent Neural Networks (HA-RNN) model. HA-RNN combined sequence modeling and attribute embedding in item recommendation. Different from conventional RNNs, HA-RNN develops a hierarchical attribute combination mechanism to deal with variable lengths of attributes. The model uses attributes in the output layer and shares the parameters with the input layer to offer additional model regularization. It takes the union of identity and attributes as a sequence element and is able to capture the global sequential dependencies between items as well as between attributes.

Smirnova et al. [16] proposed a class of Contextual RNNs(CRNNs) for recommendation that can take into account the contextual information both in the input and output layers. Their method modifies the behavior of RNN by combining the context embedding with the item embedding and explicitly parameterizing the hidden unit transitions as a function of context information in the model dynamics.

Balakrishnan et al. [17] proposed a deep-playlist generation model, which uses LSTM-RNN to predict similarity between songs. Yang et al. [18] examined three state of the art deep neural network approaches: LSTM, Encoder-Decoder and Memory network in sequence prediction field to handle the software sequence learning and prediction task. Then, modified approaches based on these state of the art models were proposed to deal with additional information in sequence. These approaches focused on adding information to enrich embedding input of LSTM-RNN, adding a classifier to encoder-decoder neural network as an assisting model and processing data to be structured for memory unit in memory network.

2.2 Collaborative Filtering-Based Recommendations Using RNN

Often, when given a number of users with a record of their history, the next specific user consumption can be predicted in one of two ways; observing that user's history in isolation or finding similar users with a close consumption pattern. We review some related work focused on the latter. Devooght et al. [4] explored the use of RNN for the collaborative filtering problem. Using RNNs, they reframed collaborative filtering as a sequence prediction problem, leading to richer models and taking the evolution of users' taste into account. Their experiments showed that the LSTM-RNNs produce very good results on the Movielens and Netflix datasets, and is especially good in terms of short term prediction and item coverage as compared to standard nearest neighbors and matrix factorization methods. Their conclusions however, was based on the vanilla LSTM-RNN, the basic form of LSTM-RNN.

Similarly, leveraging user online activity sequences, Ko et al. [6] proposed a flexible and expressive collaborative sequence model based on RNNs. The model is designed to capture a user's contextual state as a personalized hidden vector by summarizing cues from a data-driven, thus variable, number of past time steps, and representing items by a real-valued embedding. They found that, by exploiting the inherent structure in the data, their formulation led to an efficient and practical method.

Another example of collaborative filtering-based sequence modeling can be seen in the work of Bansal et al. [19]. In their paper, they presented a method leveraging deep RNNs to encode a text sequence into a latent vector. GRUs were trained end-to-end to carry out the collaborative filtering task. In their application case study of scientific paper recommendation, the GRU training yielded models with significantly higher accuracy. Performance was further improved by multi-task learning, where the text encoder network is trained for a combination of content recommendation and item meta-data prediction.

2.3 Personalized Recommendation Using RNN

In the area of personalized recommendation Wu et al. [20], in their paper, outlined how they built a deep RNN (DRNN) to address the problem of collaborative filtering's failure to exploit current viewing history of the user which leads to an inability to provide a real-time customized recommendation. Their network tracks how users browse the website using multiple hidden layers. Each hidden layer models how the combinations of web pages are accessed and in what order. They developed an optimizer to automatically tune the parameters of their neural network to achieve a better performance. Their results on real world dataset showed that the DRNN approach outperforms previous collaborative filtering approaches significantly.

Donkers et al. [7] proposed how individual users can be represented in addition to sequences of consumed items in a new type of GRU, to effectively produce personalized next item recommendations. First, they used GRU-RNN to model the temporal dynamics of consumption sequences. Then, through a gated architecture with additional input layers, they explicitly represented an individual user. Their user-based GRUs were uniquely designed and optimized for the purpose of generating personalized next item recommendations.

Quadrana et al. [21] addressed the challenge of personalizing session-based recommendation by proposing a model based Hierarchical RNN (HRNN). Their HRNN model builds extra features on top of the standard RNN. First, there is an additional GRU layer to model information across user sessions and to track the evolution of the user interests over time. Also incorporated is a user-parallel mini-batch mechanism for efficient training.

To make the most out of encoder-decoder LSTM-RNNs, our methods in this work stand out from all of the above related works especially in how we practically capture and model the consumption complexities of the users for personalized recommendation. We build a very unique strong coherence between the various user events in each unique user consumption sequence. This especially

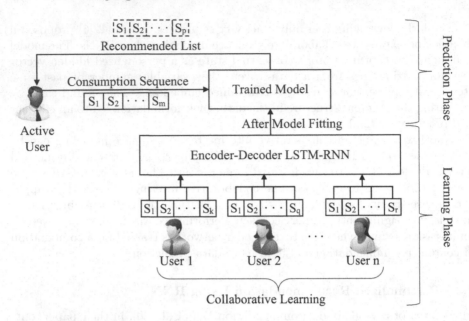

Fig. 1. Overview of the proposed collaborative learning model for personalized recommendation

helps different user patterns to be loosely coupled with each other, thereby better differentiating between unique user consumption patterns resulting in a more user aware model to improve personalized recommendation.

3   LSTM-RNN Based Collaborative Learning Model

In this section, we progressively give a detailed description of our proposed collaborative learning model for personalized recommendation. Figure 1 gives an overview of our proposed collaborative learning model for personalized recommendation. As shown in Fig. 1, our model comprises two main phases: learning phase and the prediction phase. In the learning phase, the timestamped user consumption sequence of a number of users are collated and fed into an encoder-decoder LSTM-RNN for model fitting to begin. After model fitting is complete, the trained model is now ready to make predictions based on user consumption sequences. With the fitted model, we feed in the consumption sequence of an active user to generate a list of items to be recommend. Section 3.2 discusses the technical details of our model.

Given a number of users and their item consumption history, how best can we make a personalized recommendation list of items to a specific user? As a case study, in this work, we use movies from the Movielens dataset as the item of consumption in question. Our quest, now, is to make a personalized movie recommendation for any user of our choice, based on the user's consumption history.

3.1 Problem Definition

Formally, let $\mathcal{U} = \{u_1, u_2, ..., u_n\}$ be a set of users and $\mathcal{S} = \{s_1, s_2, ..., s_m\}$ be a set of services. We assume the number of users and services to be fixed. For each user $u \in \mathcal{U}$, we associate a consumption sequence $\mathcal{CS}(u) = [cs_{t_0}^u, cs_{t_1}^u, ..., cs_{t_k}^u]$, where each $cs_{t_k}^u \in \mathcal{S}$ and $t_0 \prec t_1 \prec ... \prec t_k$ denotes the time sequence of the service invocations. It must be noted that each service invocation in u's consumption sequence is an exclusive choice over $\mathcal{S}$. In addition, we focus on the consumption sequences to exploit the temporal order implicit in user consumption events.

Given a set of consumption sequences, $\mathcal{C} = \{\mathcal{CS}(u_1), \mathcal{CS}(u_2), ..., \mathcal{CS}(u_n)\}$ and a collaborative learning model $\mathfrak{L}$, we obtain a predictive model, $\mathfrak{P}$, after $\mathfrak{L}$ has learned on $\mathcal{C}$ over a period of time.

$$\mathfrak{L}(\mathcal{C}) :\longrightarrow \mathfrak{P} \tag{1}$$

Let a be an active user, such that $a \in \mathcal{U}$, with a consumption sequence, $\mathcal{CS}(a)$, we can predict the next p consumption sequence of a, using $\mathfrak{P}$.

3.2 Personalized Encoder-Decoder LSTM-RNN

The LSTM. Long Short-Term Memory (LSTM) networks are a special kind of Recurrent Neural Network (RNN), capable of learning long-term dependencies. They were introduced by Hochreiter and Schmidhuber [22] to address the vanishing gradient and exploding gradient issues in RNN, when the number of items in the sequence gets large (long term dependencies). Figure 2 shows a schematic diagram of a single LSTM block. An LSTM is composed of a cell, an input gate, an output gate and a forget gate. The major component is the cell state ("memory") which runs through the entire chain with occasional information updates from the input(add) and forget(remove) gates. An LSTM network computes a mapping from an input sequence $x = (x_1, ..., x_T)$ to an output sequence $y = (y_1, ..., y_T)$ by calculating the network unit activations using the following equations iteratively from $t = 1\,to\,T$ [23]:

$$i_t = \sigma(W_{ix}x_t + W_{im}m_{t-1} + W_{ic}c_t + b_i) \tag{2}$$

$$f_t = \sigma(W_{fx}x_t + W_{fm}m_{t-1} + W_{fc}c_{t-1} + b_f) \tag{3}$$

$$c_t = f_t \odot c_{t-1} + i_t \odot g(W_{cx}x_t + W_{cm}m_{t-1} + b_c) \tag{4}$$

$$o_t = \sigma(w_{ox}x_t + W_{om}m_{t-1} + W_{oc}c_t + b_o) \tag{5}$$

$$m_t = o_t \odot h(c_t) \tag{6}$$

$$y_t = \phi(W_{ym}m_t + b_y) \tag{7}$$

- f: forget gate's activation vector
- i: input gate's activation vector
- o: output gate's activation vector
- h: output vector of the LSTM unit

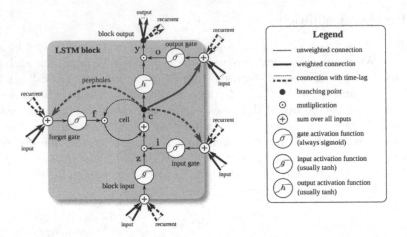

Fig. 2. Detailed schematic of an LSTM block as used in the hidden layers of a recurrent neural network [24]

- g: cell input activation function, generally tanh
- h: cell output activation functions, generally tanh
- c: cell activation vector
- W: weight matrices parameters
- b: bias vector parameters
- $\odot$: element-wise product of the vectors
- σ: the logistic sigmoid function
- ϕ: the network output activation function

The Encoder-Decoder. Figure 3 shows a simplified model of the encoder-decoder network architecture. An encoder is a network that takes the input and encodes it into an internal representation (feature/context vector), that holds the information and features, which best represents the input. The decoder is also a network that uses the vector from the encoder to generate an output sequence. In general, these networks only predict probabilities and the idea here is to first calculate the initial state of the input into a hidden state which is fed to the decoder to decode the information into the output sequence. A *softmax* takes the decoder's hidden state at time step t, and translates it into probability.

Our Model: The Personalized Encoder-Decoder LSTM-RNN. To prepare the data for training and subsequent testing, the input and expected output strings are tokenized into integers and the respective tokenizers are trained for our model. The encoded integers are then padded to the maximum input and output lengths respectively and the output sequence is one-hot encoded. We employ the encoder-decoder LSTM architecture to recommend a list of items for a user, based on his/her consumption preference. The choice of LSTM stems

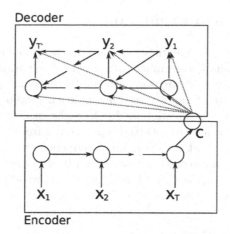

Fig. 3. A simplified illustration of an LSTM Encoder Decoder [25]

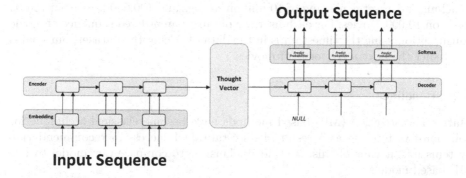

Fig. 4. Encoder-Decoder set-up for our experiments

from the fact that a comprehensive model and relationship will be learned from the user's consumption preference as well as the consumption preference of similar users thus introducing long-term dependencies [22]. The encoder-decoder architecture helps us to recommend a list of items to the user based on his/her consumption history and/or the consumption history of similar users. Figure 4 shows the basic set-up we used for our experiments. The encoder is basically a stack of LSTM cells. The thought vector is the final hidden state of the encoder. The actual outputs from the encoder are not passed to the decoder but rather the final hidden state. The decoder is also a stack of LSTM cells. The initial states of the decoder are set to the final states of the encoder. The model is trained using cross-entropy loss. At each step, the network produces a probability distribution over possible next tokens. The parameters for the model are carefully selected to provide the best training and subsequent prediction.

4   Experiments and Evaluation

We conducted several experiments to evaluate our proposed collaborative learning model for personalized recommendation. These experiments were done to ascertain the performance of our proposed model on seq2seq recommendations compared to other state of the art recommendation methods. Specifically, We considered a variation of our collaborative learning model where input to the encoder is reversed. The idea of reversed input comes from Sutskever et al. [11], where their tests proved that reversing input sequence presents some benefits to the model. In addition, we considered two variants of matrix factorization (MF) methods; Bayesian Personalized Ranking Matrix Factorization [8] and Adaptive Hinge Pairwise Matrix Factorization [9].

4.1   Dataset Description

We used the publicly available Movielens 10M[1] dataset. Movielens dataset is a benchmark dataset consisting of 10 million ratings and 100,000 tags from 72,000 users on 10,000 Movies. For each user, we obtained an ordered sequence of movie consumption using the timestamps in the dataset. Using the dataset, our goal is to predict the next n sequence of movies.

4.2   Baselines

Matrix Factorization (MF)-based methods have become classical technique for collaborative filtering as a result of its established success in recommendation systems [6]. In view of this, we find it plausible to compare our model to two MF based models.

- **Bayesian Personalized ranking Matrix Factorization (BPR-MF):** BPR-MF is a state of the art MF method for recommending Top-N items [4]. It is based on Bayesian Personalized Ranking loss function.
- **Adaptive Hinge Matrix Factorization (AHP-MF):** AHP-MF is based on the Adaptive hinge pairwise loss function (AHP). The AHP loss, in the SpotLight library, is an approximation for the Weighted Approximate-Rank Pairwise (WARP) loss scheme, proposed by Weston et al. [9]. According to Weston et al. [9], WARP loss yields better performance. For its competitiveness, we decided to consider AHP Matrix Factorization as one of our baselines.

---

[1] https://grouplens.org/datasets/movielens.

4.3   Metrics

The following metrics were chosen:

- **Recall:** Recall refers to sensitivity of the model. It captures the effectiveness of the model in terms of outputting relevant predictions. It can be computed as:

$$Recall(W_i) = \frac{tPositive(W_i)}{tPositive(W_i) + fNegative(W_i)}$$

- **Precision:** It assesses the predictive power of the algorithm [26].

$$Precision(W_i) = \frac{tPositive(W_i)}{tPositive(W_i) + fPositive(W_i)}$$

- **F-Measure:** This is defined on both recall and precision. It could be viewed as the weighted average of recall and precision. It rewards higher sensitivity [26].

$$F - Measure = 2 \times \frac{Precision \times Recall}{Precision + Recall}$$

Where $tPositive$, $fPositive$ and $fNegative$ are true positive, false positive and false negative respectively. Higher precision, recall and F-measure values indicates better performance.

4.4   Results and Discussions

We applied our method to the consumption preferences of 5000 users from the movielens dataset which translates into a combination of 625,000 different consumption preferences. In this section, we compare the results from our model with the results from the baselines described in the previous section.

Our main aim was to recommend a list of items (in this case, movies) to a user, based on what he has previously consumed and what other similar users have consumed. By similar users, we are referring to users who have similar consumption preferences and therefore are more likely to have similar future preferences.

All our LSTM models were fed with user consumption one after the other into the encoder and a sequence of outputs are obtained from the decoder. Details of the setup of our experiments are listed below:

1. 127,000 user consumption preferences with an encoder-decoder setup, both with a hidden state of 256 units. We trained the network over 20 epochs while updating the parameters using Adam optimization.
2. Input to encoder is reversed, 127,000 user consumption preferences with an encoder-decoder setup, both with a hidden state of 256 units. We trained the network over 20 epochs while updating the parameters using Adam optimization.
3. 625,000 user consumption preferences with an encoder-decoder setup, both with a hidden state of 256 units. We trained the network over 15 epochs while updating the parameters using Adam optimization.

Table 1. Training (Model) Parameters

Models	Learning_rate	Loss	Epochs	Batch	Emb_Dim	Optimizer
BPR-MF	0.05	bpr	10	256	32	ADAM
AHP-MF	0.01	Adaptive_Hinge	10	256	32	ADAM

4. Input to encoder is reversed, 625,000 user consumption preferences with an encoder-decoder setup, both with a hidden state of 256 units. We trained the network over 15 epochs while updating the parameters using Adam optimization. Table 1 shows the training parameters used for our baselines.

We evaluate the results of our experiments in terms of Recall@10, Precision@10 and F-Measure@10. Recall@k is equivalent to the hit-rate metric [21], and it measures the proportion of cases out of all test cases in which the relevant item is amongst the top-k items. This is an accurate model for certain practical scenarios where no recommendation is highlighted and their absolute order does not matter. Precision@k measures the fraction of correct recommendations in the top-k positions of each recommendation list. The training and validation accuracies from our experiments are captured in Figs. 5 and 6.

As expected, our experiments showed that increasing the number of users from 1000 to 5000 has a significant effect on the overall performance of the model. This shows that the collaboration from other users actually helps to improve the performance of our model by 27%. We also observed that reversing the input data gave an extra boost to the performance by a 14% margin. This shows that the idea of collaborative learning for personalized recommendation helps improve recommendation accuracy by a great deal.

From Table 2 BPR-MF had quite a good score (10%) in terms of precision as compared to AHP-MF. It was observed that the Adaptive Model (AHP-MF) produced low outputs, approximately 4.89% on recall, 7.26% precision and 5.84% F-measure.

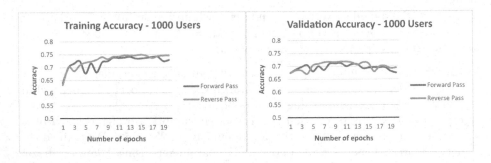

Fig. 5. A plot of training and validation accuracies for 1000 users

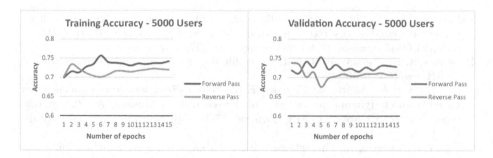

Fig. 6. A plot of training and validation accuracies for 5000 users

Table 2. Recall@k, Precision@k and F-Measure@k, (where k=10) on Movielens dataset

Model	Recall	Precision	F-Measure
BPR-MF	0.0679	0.1021	0.0816
AHP-MF	0.0489	0.0726	0.0584
Encoder-Decoder (1000 Users)	0.2068	0.2074	0.2071
Encoder-Decoder (1000 Users Reverse)	0.2454	0.2461	0.2457
Encoder-Decoder (5000 Users)	0.2723	0.2731	0.2727
Encoder-Decoder (5000 Users Reverse)	**0.2998**	**0.3006**	**0.3002**

5   Conclusions and Future Work

In this paper, we built a user consumption-sensitive Long Short-Term Memory recurrent neural network; specifically, an encoder-decoder model to tackle the real world problem of sequence to sequence prediction. Our model helped us to bridge the gap and benefit from the desirable attributes of both personalized recommendations based solely on a user's consumption history, and generic recommendation which is based on collaborative filtering. We have demonstrated that our method can significantly outperform popular baselines that are used for this task. We also noticed that the format in which the data is modeled has a very big impact on the performance of the network. In the near future, we will work on various data modeling formats and analyze which one is best suited for what purpose.

References

1. Quadrana, M., Cremonesi, P., Jannach, D.: Sequence-aware recommender systems. CoRR abs/1802.08452 (2018)
2. Fletcher, K.K.: A method for dealing with data sparsity and cold-start limitations in service recommendation using personalized preferences. In: 2017 IEEE International Conference on Cognitive Computing (ICCC), pp. 72–79, June 2017

3. Fletcher, K.K., Liu, X.F.: A collaborative filtering method for personalized preference-based service recommendation. In: Proceedings of the 2015 IEEE International Conference on Web Services, pp. 400–407, June 2015

4. Devooght, R., Bersini, H.: Collaborative filtering with recurrent neural networks. CoRR abs/1608.07400 (2016)

5. Kwapong, B.A., Anarfi, R., Fletcher, K.K.: Personalized service recommendation based on user dynamic preferences. In: Ferreira, J.E., Musaev, A., Zhang, L.J. (eds.) Services Computing - SCC 2019, pp. 77–91. Springer International Publishing, Cham (2019)

6. Ko, Y.J., Maystre, L., Grossglauser, M.: Collaborative recurrent neural networks for dynamic recommender systems. In: Journal of Machine Learning Research: Workshop and Conference Proceedings, vol. 63 (2016)

7. Donkers, T., Loepp, B., Ziegler, J.: Sequential user-based recurrent neural network recommendations. In: Proceedings of the Eleventh ACM Conference on Recommender Systems, pp. 152–160. ACM (2017)

8. Rendle, S., Freudenthaler, C., Gantner, Z., Schmidt-Thieme, L.: BPR: Bayesian personalized ranking from implicit feedback. In: Proceedings of the Twenty-Fifth Conference on Uncertainty in Artificial Intelligence, pp. 452–461. AUAI Press (2009)

9. Weston, J., Bengio, S., Usunier, N.: WSABIE: scaling up to large vocabulary image annotation. IJCAI 11, 2764–2770 (2011)

10. Park, S., Kim, B., Kang, C.M., Chung, C.C., Choi, J.W.: Sequence-to-sequence prediction of vehicle trajectory via LSTM encoder-decoder architecture. arXiv preprint arXiv:1802.06338 (2018)

11. Sutskever, I., Vinyals, O., Le, Q.V.: Sequence to sequence learning with neural networks. In: Advances in Neural Information Processing Systems, pp. 3104–3112 (2014)

12. Vinyals, O., Kaiser, L., Koo, T., Petrov, S., Sutskever, I., Hinton, G.: Grammar as a foreign language. In: Advances in Neural Information Processing Systems, pp. 2773–2781 (2015)

13. Chu, Y., Huang, F., Wang, H., Li, G., Song, X.: Short-term recommendation with recurrent neural networks. In: 2017 IEEE International Conference on Mechatronics and Automation (ICMA), pp. 927–932. IEEE (2017)

14. Hidasi, B., Karatzoglou, A., Baltrunas, L., Tikk, D.: Session-based recommendations with recurrent neural networks. arXiv preprint arXiv:1511.06939 (2015)

15. Liu, K., Shi, X., Natarajan, P.: Sequential heterogeneous attribute embedding for item recommendation. In: 2017 IEEE International Conference on Data Mining Workshops (ICDMW), pp. 773–780, November 2017

16. Smirnova, E., Vasile, F.: Contextual sequence modeling for recommendation with recurrent neural networks. arXiv preprint arXiv:1706.07684 (2017)

17. Balakrishnan, A., Dixit, K.: DeepPlaylist: using recurrent neural networks to predict song similarity (2016)

18. Yang, Q., He, Z., Ge, F., Zhang, Y.: Sequence-to-sequence prediction of personal computer software by recurrent neural network. In: 2017 International Joint Conference on Neural Networks (IJCNN), pp. 934–940, May 2017

19. Bansal, T., Belanger, D., McCallum, A.: Ask the GRU: multi-task learning for deep text recommendations. In: Proceedings of the 10th ACM Conference on Recommender Systems, pp. 107–114. ACM (2016)

20. Wu, S., Ren, W., Yu, C., Chen, G., Zhang, D., Zhu, J.: Personal recommendation using deep recurrent neural networks in NetEase. In: 2016 IEEE 32nd International Conference on Data Engineering (ICDE), pp. 1218–1229.IEEE (2016)

21. Quadrana, M., Karatzoglou, A., Hidasi, B., Cremonesi, P.: Personalizing session-based recommendations with hierarchical recurrent neural networks. In: Proceedings of the Eleventh ACM Conference on Recommender Systems, pp. 130–137. ACM (2017)
22. Hochreiter, S., Schmidhuber, J.: Long short-term memory. Neural Comput. **9**(8), 1735–1780 (1997)
23. Sak, H., Senior, A., Beaufays, F.: Long short-term memory recurrent neural network architectures for large scale acoustic modeling. In: Fifteenth Annual Conference of the International Speech Communication Association (2014)
24. Greff, K., Srivastava, R.K., Koutník, J., Steunebrink, B.R., Schmidhuber, J.: LSTM: a search space odyssey. IEEE Trans. Neural Netw. Learn. Syst. **28**(10), 2222–2232 (2017)
25. Cho, K., et al.: Learning phrase representations using RNN encoder-decoder for statistical machine translation. arXiv preprint arXiv:1406.1078 (2014)
26. Sokolova, M., Japkowicz, N., Szpakowicz, S.: Beyond accuracy, F-Score and ROC: a family of discriminant measures for performance evaluation. In: Sattar, A., Kang, B. (eds.) AI 2006. LNCS (LNAI), vol. 4304, pp. 1015–1021. Springer, Heidelberg (2006). https://doi.org/10.1007/11941439_114

An Attention Model for Mashup Tag Recommendation

Kenneth K. Fletcher$^{(\boxtimes)}$ (iD)

University of Massachusetts Boston, Boston, MA 02125, USA
kenneth.fletcher@umb.edu

Abstract. Mashups have emerged as a popular technique to compose value-added web services/APIs, to fulfill some complicated business needs. This has increased the number of available mashups over the internet. The increase however, poses a new requirement of organizing and managing these mashups for better understanding and discovery. For this reason, tags have become highly important because they describe items and allows for easy discovery. Most existing tag recommendation methods typically follow a manual process based on controlled vocabulary, or consider tags as words in isolation contained in mashup descriptions. Such methods therefore fail to characterize the diverse functional features of mashups. This work proposes an attention model to automatically recommend mashup tags. Specifically, our proposed model has two levels of attention mechanisms applied at the word- and sentence-levels and subsequently recommend top-N words with highest attention weights as tags. Our model is based on the intuition that not every word in a mashup description is equally relevant in identifying its functional aspects. Therefore, determining the relevant sections involves modeling the interactions of the words, not just their presence in isolation. We demonstrate the effectiveness of our method by conducting extensive experiments on a real-world dataset crawled from www.programmableweb.com. We also compare our method with some baseline tag recommendation methods for verification.

Keywords: Mashup · Tags · Tag recommendation · Attention mechanism · GRU · Mashup development

1 Introduction

Mashups represent a type of lightweight Web applications that compose several existing Web APIs or services in an agile manner, to meet users' complex application needs [1,2]. The benefits of the mashup technology has increased its demand and consequently, the number of mashups available in online repositories like www.programmableweb.com. For instance, over the past few years, the number of mashups on www.programmableweb.com has increased rapidly by almost 200% to 7,953, belonging to more than 430 predefined categories, as at October 2019 [3]. With this much mashups, developers are now faced with

Q. Wang et al. (Eds.): SCC 2020, LNCS 12409, pp. 50–64, 2020.
https://doi.org/10.1007/978-3-030-59592-0_4

the challenge of organizing and managing these mashups for better understanding of their functionalities and discovery. Among all the different techniques of organizing and managing web services, tagging is widely known to be an efficient technique [4]. Tagging is the way of annotating services with some meaningful terms, in order to capture their functionalities based on their service descriptions.

Existing methods to automatically recommend tags for traditional web services are typically based on topic-modeling [5–7] and clustering [6,8]. Although such tag recommendation techniques are effective in recommending tags for traditional web services, their application to recommending tags for mashups is limited. This is because:

1. Mashup descriptions are typically short (empirical study discussed in Sect. 2.1 revealed 2–3 sentences on an average). For this reason, topic-modeling based methods like LDA will fail to identify functionally related tags because they suffer from low efficiency, excessive long training time and low accuracy, especially in applications where the input document is relatively short [1,9],
2. the potentially inaccurate representations of mashup functionalities learned by the topic models will introduce the intention gap limitation during similarity computation of functional descriptions of mashups [6], and
3. Such methods fail to recommend accurate tags because they do not model the interactions between words but rather consider their presence in isolation [10].

On the other hand, there are few existing works that have proposed methods specific to recommend tags for mashups. These methods are either (1) a manual process that is based on controlled vocabulary, like the current tag recommender system on www.programmableweb.com (see Sect. 2.1). (2) based on learned interactions between mashups and web APIs [4]. Since mashups have different functionalities than their constituent web APIs, such methods will miss newer terms used to describe a particular mashup or recommend redundant or similar tags thereby failing to uncover the new functionalities of a mashup. Therefore, there is the need for a method to recommend mashup tags that overcomes the above limitations in order to accurately recommend tags that reveals the value-added functionalities in mashup descriptions.

In this paper, we propose just such a method for mashup tag recommendation. Our proposed method employs attention mechanism in natural language processing (NLP), to learn the interactions between words in mashup description in order to reveal the functional properties in those descriptions. Specifically, we first train a vector representation of words using web APIs and mashup descriptions. Then using this trained embeddings, we train an attention model to learn the interactions between the words in a mashup description. The attention model assigns weights to each word in the mashup description. We finally recommend top-N words with highest weights as mashup tags.

To sum up, the contributions of this work are in threefold:

1. We employ the GloVe [11] word embedding framework to train a word embedding model by integrating web API and mashup descriptions into existing corpus. By training on web API and mashup data, our model reduces the issue of out-of-vocabulary words, inherent with word embedding models.
2. We employ the hierarchical attention model [10] to accurately recommend tags for mashups. Typically, the same word or sentence may have different importance in different context. In order to capture this notion, our model includes both word - and sentence - levels of attention mechanisms [12,13]. This technique will allow our model to pay more or less attention to individual words and sentences when constructing the representation of the mashup description.
3. We conduct extensive experiments to evaluate and validate our proposed method against state of the art methods using a collection of 6,270 mashups from www.programmableweb.com [1,2].

The rest of this paper is organized as follows: In Sect. 2, we present our findings on an empirical study on mashup dataset and give some background information about word embeddings and attention mechanism in NLP. We present our proposed method in detail in Sect. 3, followed by our experiments, evaluations and results analysis in Sect. 4. In Sect. 5 we discuss some of the current state-of-the-art mashup tag recommendation works. Finally, we conclude our paper and discuss some directions for our future work in Sect. 6.

2   Background

In this section we give some background information relating to our proposed method. First, we present our findings on an empirical study we conducted on a mashup dataset from www.programmableweb.com. We subsequently give a brief description of word embeddings and attention in NLP and how they are used in our work.

2.1   Empirical Study

We study one of the popular online web APIs and mashups repository, www.programmableweb.com, which is by far the largest online web APIs repository that contains over 19,000 web APIs and 6,270 mashups with various functionalities [1–3]. We crawled web APIs, mashups and user profiles from this online web API repository and analyzed the mashup descriptions and tags. Table 1 shows details of the crawled dataset. Each web API is described by fields such as an ID, short description, primary and secondary categories, number of developers and followers, and much more. Similarly, for the mashup dataset, each mashup is described by an ID, description, primary and secondary categories, tags, related web APIs, date mashup was created and so on.

Generally, mashup descriptions are very short. According to our study, on an average, there are 3 sentences in a mashup description and 17 words in a

Table 1. Statistical information of the dataset

Item type	Number
Number of Web APIs	17,564
Number of Mashups	6,270
Number of User Profiles	87,857
User-Web API Invocation Matrix Density	2.2159×10^{-6}
User-Web API Interaction Matrix Density	1.1417×10^{-5}

sentence. In addition, only a small portion of the words in a mashup description are functionally related and they are usually the most reliable information responsible for accurate tag recommendation. Figure 1 for instance, shows an example mashup from www.programmableweb.com. For this mashup, there are 3 tags, and a description with 2 sentences. Also, it can be seen that the main words that are functionally related are **find**, **bank**, **location**, and **search**.

We also studied mashup tags from our dataset. We observed that tagging of mashups are typically a manual process that uses some pre-defined controlled vocabulary. For instance, in our example mashup in Fig. 1, *Mapping*, *Banking*, and *Financial* are the tags for the mashup. These words are also the pre-defined categories used to categorize mashups. Although using controlled vocabulary for tagging helps retrieve all the items tagged under a particular topic, it is easy to miss newer terms and jargon/slang used to describe a particular functionality in a mashup description. For this specific mashup example in Fig. 1, we can argue that **searching** is a functionality of this mashup as depicted by words like **find** and **search**, present in the description. However, due to the use of controlled vocabulary for tagging, **find** and **search** were not selected as tags. Therefore in order to provide flexible mashup discovery and management, we propose a method to automatically recommend tags for mashups.

2.2   Word Embedding

Word embeddings are basically a form of word representation that bridges the human understanding of language to that of a machine [14]. Word embeddings are dense, semantically-meaningful and distributed representations of text in an

Fig. 1. An example mashup from www.programmableweb.com

n-dimensional space which becomes essential for solving most NLP problems. By embedding words by some low-dimensional vectors, we can capture the semantic relevance between words in context. Word embedding techniques are popular these days because they overcome the limitations of on-hot encoding words such as similarity, vocabulary size and computational issues. The importance of word embeddings in the field of deep learning is evidenced by the numerous researches that leverage it. One such research in the field of word embeddings is GloVe [11], which we employ to embed words in our proposed method.

2.3 Attention Mechanism

Attention has been a popular concept and a useful tool in the deep learning community in recent years. To some extent, it is motivated by how we pay visual attention to different regions of an image or correlate words in one sentence [15]. It can be employed to explain the relationship between words in one sentence or close context. For instance in the mashup description in Fig. 1, when we see **help**, we expect to encounter a need word like **find** very soon. Attention in the deep learning can be broadly interpreted as a vector of importance weights. That is, in order to predict or infer an element (target element), such as a word in a sentence, we need to estimate how strongly it is correlated with ("attends to") other elements. We then approximate the target element by taking the sum of their values weighted by the attention vector. In our work, we employ this mechanism to find the interactions between words in a mashup description in order to reveal the functional aspects of the mashup. We subsequently recommend words with higher weights as mashup tags.

3   Attention Model for Mashup Tag Recommendation

The proposed model for mashup tag recommendation is shown in Fig. 2. The input to our trained network is a mashup description and the output of the network is a mashup description vector containing both sentence and word weights. We recommend top-N words with highest weights as tags for the mashup.

Formally, let $D = \{s_1, s_2, .., s_L\}$ be a mashup description of a new mashup m', made up of L sentences (s) and each sentence $s = \{w_1, w_2, .., w_T\}$ consist of T words (w). For each word w_{it} in an ith sentence, where $t \in [1, T]$, we learn an embedding x_{it} using the GloVe embedding model $\mathcal{E}$ [11] such that:

$$x_{it} = \mathcal{E}(w_{it}), t \in [1, T] \tag{1}$$

where x_{it} is the embedded vector of w_{it}. We seek to find a learning model $\mathcal{L}$, that can learn the attention weights of both words and sentences in D, using the embedded vectors x_{it}, such that

$$\mathcal{L}(D) :\longrightarrow \{w'_{it}...\} \tag{2}$$

The mashup tag recommendation problem can be formulated as given a new mashup m' with description D, we want to automatically recommend some relevant tags $G = \{g_1, g_2, .., g_n\}$ with $G \in D$, that can characterize the functional properties of m', where G is ranked based on the learned weights.

Our proposed attention model for mashup tag recommendation has 3 main components: *Word Embedding*, *Word-Level Attention*, and *Sentence-Level Attention*. We discuss each of these components and our entire network in detail in the sections that follow.

3.1 GloVe Word Embeddings

Global Vectors (GloVe) is an unsupervised learning algorithm for obtaining vector representations for words [11]. Training is performed on aggregated global word-word co-occurrence statistics from a corpus, and the resulting representations showcase interesting linear substructures of the word vector space. GloVe is essentially a log-bilinear model with a weighted least-squares objective. The main intuition underlying the model is the simple observation that ratios of word-word co-occurrence probabilities have the potential for encoding some form of meaning. The goal of Glove is very straightforward, i.e., to enforce the word vectors to capture sub-linear relationships in the vector space. Although there are many word embedding techniques, we employ GloVe to learn word embeddings for our proposed model because it proves to perform better than others in the word analogy tasks. This is because, Glove adds practical meaning into word vectors by considering the relationships between word pairs rather than words in isolation. Finally, Glove gives lower weight for highly frequent word pairs so as to prevent frequency of a word to dominate the training progress.

We included web API and mashup descriptions from our dataset into an available corpus to train our word embeddings. We did this in order to learn the vector representations of words used to describe the functional properties of mashups and web APIs. This was necessary in order to reduce out-of-vocabulary words.

3.2 Word-Level Attention

The word-level attention mechanism consist of two main parts: (1) a bi-directional gated recurrent unit (GRU) encoder which learns and returns relevant word contexts, and (2) an attention mechanism that learns and computes a vector of importance weights for each word context.

Bi-directional GRU encoder. For each embedded word x_{it}, we use a bi-directional GRU encoder to extract relevant contexts of every sentence $s_t \in D$. By using a bi-directional GRU we can get annotations of words by summarizing information from both forward GRU, $\overrightarrow{GRU}$ which reads a sentence s_t from w_{i1} to w_{iT} and a backward GRU, $\overleftarrow{GRU}$ which reads s_t from w_{iT} to w_{i1}, resulting in a summarized variable h_{it}.

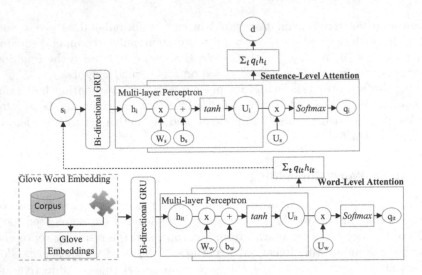

Fig. 2. Overview of the proposed attention model for mashup tag recommendation.

$$\overrightarrow{h_{it}} = \overrightarrow{GRU}(x_{it}), t \in [1, T]$$
$$\overleftarrow{h_{it}} = \overleftarrow{GRU}(x_{it}), t \in [T, 1] \qquad (3)$$
$$h_{it} = [\overrightarrow{h_{it}}, \overleftarrow{h_{it}}]$$

Word Attention. Not all words contribute equally to the representation of the sentence meaning. Hence, we introduce attention mechanism to extract such words that are important to the meaning of the sentence and aggregate the representation of those informative words to form a sentence vector [10]. The attention mechanism at the word-level consist of one-layer multi-layer perceptron (MLP). The goal of this layer is to learn through training with randomly initialized weights (W) and biases (b). The layer uses the *tanh* function to ensure that the network does not falter. The *tanh* function achieves this by correcting input values to be between -1 and 1 and also maps zeros to near-zero. The input to this layer are the word annotations h_{it} with another hidden layer. These annotations are subsequently improved by the word weights, W_w and word biases, b_w as

$$u_{it} = tanh(W_w h_{it} + b_w) \qquad (4)$$

We jointly train a word context vector u_w which is randomly initialized. The jointly learned context vector u_w is then multiplied with the new annotations, u_{it} and subsequently normalized to an importance weight per word α_{it} by a *softmax* function as

$$\alpha_{it} = \frac{exp(u_{it}^T, u_w)}{\sum_t exp(u_{it}^T, u_w)} \qquad (5)$$

Finally, we sum these importance weights, concatenated with the previously calculated context annotations, h_{it} to obtain the sentence vector s_i

$$s_i = \sum_t \alpha_{it} h_{it} \tag{6}$$

3.3 Sentence-Level Attention

In order to reward sentences that are clues to correctly projecting the functionality of a mashup description, we again use attention mechanism and introduce a sentence level context vector u_s and use the vector to measure the importance of the sentences. More concretely, the whole network for the word-level attention mechanism is run with focus on the sentences. We should note that there is no embedding layer as we already obtained the sentence vectors s_i from word-level attention as input. The bi-directional GRU encoder for the sentence-level will yield:

$$\overrightarrow{h_i} = \overrightarrow{GRU}(s_i), i \in [1, L]$$
$$\overleftarrow{h_i} = \overleftarrow{GRU}(s_i), i \in [L, 1] \tag{7}$$
$$h_i = [\overrightarrow{h_i}, \overleftarrow{h_i}]$$

Sentence Attention. Trainable weights and biases are again randomly initialized and jointly learned during the training process. The final output is a document vector d which can be used as features for mashup tag recommendation.

$$u_i = tanh(W_s h_i + b_s) \tag{8}$$

$$\alpha_i = \frac{exp(u_i^T, u_s)}{\sum_t exp(u_i^T, u_s)} \tag{9}$$

$$d = \sum_i \alpha_i h_i \tag{10}$$

where d is the mashup description vector that summarizes all the information of sentences in a mashup description.

4 Experiments

We conducted several experiments to evaluate our proposed method. These experiments were done to ascertain the performance of our proposed method on mashup tag recommendations compared to other existing recommendation methods. We discuss our experimental setup and results in this section.

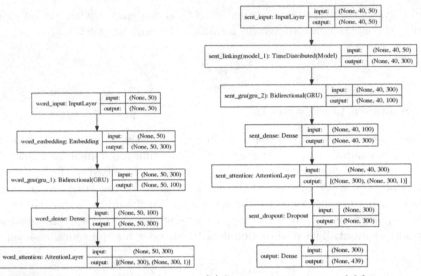

(a) Word attention model for our proposed model

(b) Sentence attention model for our proposed model

Fig. 3. Proposed models

4.1 Dataset Description

We evaluate our proposed method using web API and mashup dataset crawled from www.programmableweb.com. See Sect. 2.1 for details on the dataset. We follow a 70/10/20 proportions for splitting the original dataset into training/validation/test sets [2,16]. For each baseline, we randomly divided our dataset into five different sets of 70/10/20 proportions also representing training, validation and test respectively. We then use our proposed method to recommend tags for a new mashup. In Sect. 4.4, we present the average results from these five sets. All models were trained on the same set of hyperparameters which were tuned with the validation set. We train our model based on the parameters in Figs. 3a and b. Figures 4a and b show the accuracy and loss of our model when trained on the training parameters respectively.

4.2 Evaluation Metrics

The following were the metrics we evaluated our method against. Our choice of these metrics is purely based on the fact that they are well-known to evaluate ranking-based methods.

Recall @ K: The Recall of top-k recommendation tags is the fraction of tags among the real tag set for a mashup that are recommended. It is defined as:

$$Recall@K = \frac{|tags_{rec} \cap tags_{actual}|}{|tags_{actual}|} \tag{11}$$

Where $tags_{rec}$ is the recommended tag set, and $tags_{actual}$ is the actual tag set for the mashup.

Precision @ K: The Precision of top-k recommendation is the fraction of recommended tags that are among the real tag set for a mashup. It is defined as:

$$Precision@K = \frac{|tags_{rec} \cap tags_{actual}|}{|tags_{rec}|} \qquad (12)$$

Where $tags_{rec}$ is the recommended tag set, and $tags_{actual}$ is the actual tag set for the mashup.

F-Measure @ K: The F-Measure is a measure of the recommendation accuracy. It is the weighted harmonic mean of the precision and recall. It is defined as:

$$F - Measure@K = 2 * \frac{Precision * Recall}{Precision + Recall} \qquad (13)$$

4.3 Baselines

We compare our model to the following baseline methods to demonstrate its effectiveness.

- **Topic Sensitive Method (TSM):** this method exploits various types of relationships as features and propose a topic-sensitive approach based on Factorization Machines for mashup tag recommendation [4].
- **Mashup Tag Recommendation (MAT):** this method simultaneously incorporate the composition relationships between mashups and APIs as well as the annotation relationships between APIs and tags to discover the latent topics [17].

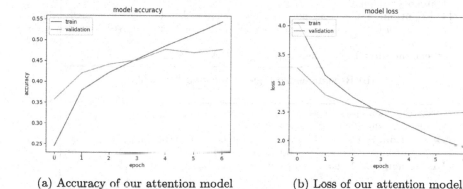

(a) Accuracy of our attention model   (b) Loss of our attention model

Fig. 4. Performance of our attention model

– **Tag-LDA:** Compared with MAT, this method takes only the annotation relationships between tags and APIs into account. The remaining recommendation steps are same as MAT.
– **Proposed Method (ATT):** This is the proposed mashup tag recommendation method in this work.

4.4 Results and Discussions

We used our trained model to recommend tags for mashups based on their descriptions. Figures 5a, b and c shows some results. Our results show that our model is able to recommend meaningful tags to mashups based on their descriptions. However, some of the tags are also not so meaningful. We attribute this to the fact that the word embedding component is not able to adequately learn words that describe the functionalities of mashup. We intend to remedy this by crawling and incorporating more text from www.programmableweb.com to learn their embeddings. Another reason why we think our model recommends not so meaningful tags sometimes is because of the short text in the mashup descriptions. We intend to leverage knowledge graphs for mashups as side information to help resolve this issue as well.

Mashup: Legacy Commemorative Guest Book
Category: Photos
Description: Uses the SharedBook Reverse Publishing Platform, multiple streams of data containing the obituary, guest book entries and family photos automatically flow from Legacy.com to SharedBook where the content is mapped into a structured book product.
Recommended Tags: ["obituary", "guest", "flow", "containing", "mapped"]

(a) Recommended tags for mashup "Legacy Commemorative Guest Book"

Mashup: Nearish
Category: Mapping
Description: Nearish.com puts you on a map with other Facebook users, allowing you to connect with people around you in realtime and "visit" others far away.
Recommended Tags: ["map", "put", "connect", "allowing", "people"]

(b) Recommended tags for mashup "Nerish"

Mashup: Open Stock Photography
Category: Education
Description: Free searchable collection of stock photography powered by Wikimedia Commons. New speed-dial number is added.
Recommended Tags: ["photography", "new", "wikimedia", "searchable", "free"]

(c) Recommended tags for mashup "Open Stock Photography"

Fig. 5. Some results from our proposed model.

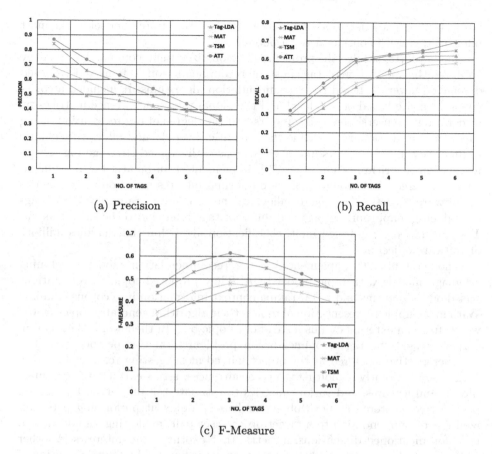

(a) Precision   (b) Recall

(c) F-Measure

Fig. 6. Performance of our model against other baselines

We also performed a performance comparison of our proposed model with other baselines. Figure 6 shows the results with respect to recall, precision, and F-Measure. From the results in the figure, we can see that besides precision @ 6, our proposed model outperformed all other baselines. Overall, the average F-Measure of our proposed model shows significant improvements over all other baseline models as follows: 4.7% over TSM, 23.3% over MAT, and 24.2% over Tag-LDA.

5 Related Work

Several works have been proposed for tag recommendation. In their paper, Shi et al. [4,17] proposed an automatic mashup tag recommendation model. It simultaneously incorporated the composition relationships between mashups and APIs as well as the annotation relationships between APIs and tags to discover the latent topics. They developed a tag filtering algorithm to further select the most relevant tags with consideration of popularity.

Yin et al. [18] tackled the problem of personalized tag recommendation. They analyzed the application of Tags in social recommendation systems and proposed diversified coverage based tag recommendation algorithms. It included a correlation measure based on the local and the global tag co-occurrence matrices by integrating the users' personal interests and the degree of tag recognition, using the WordNet dictionary to define the semantic diversity and alleviate semantic redundancy in their results and a greedy based diversified coverage tag recommendation algorithm. Zhou et al. [19] implemented automatic tag recommendation in large-scale evolving software information sites based on the semantics of software objects. This was to alleviate the problem of rapid growth of tags by reducing inappropriate tags and different tags referring to the same content. They proposed a tag-based multi-classification algorithm that handles millions of software objects.

Zhong et al. [20] implemented a tag recommendation model, combining language models with topic model LDA. They proposed topic representations based on Skip-grams and LDA, taking context information into corpus training. With measurable representation of topics, their algorithm generates topic-related words from an external corpus instead of a topic bag. In their work, Belem et al. [21] addressed the tag recommendation problem from two perspectives. The first perspective, centered at the object, aimed at suggesting relevant tags to a target object, jointly exploiting tag co-occurrences, terms extracted from multiple textual features, and various metrics to estimate tag relevance. The second perspective, centered at both object and user, aimed at performing personalized tag recommendation to a target object-user pair, exploiting, in addition to the aforementioned dimensions, a metric that captures user interests. Another content-based approach in [22] suggest tags according to the text description of a resource. By considering both the description and tags of a given resource as summaries to the resource written in two languages, they adopted word alignment models in statistical machine translation to bridge their vocabulary gap. Based on the translation probabilities between the words in descriptions and the tags estimated on a large set of description-tags pairs, they built a word trigger method (WTM) to suggest tags according to the words in a resource description. This group of methods ignore the semantic ambiguity of tags, hence the recommendation results are somewhat unsatisfactory [23,24].

Co-occurrence based methods explore tag co-occurrences to expand tag set of documents as done in [21] and [25], where they approached the problem from a demand-driven basis according to an initial set of tags applied to an object. By so doing, it reduces the space of possible solutions, so that its complexity increases polynomially with the size of the tag vocabulary. This approach however, only exploits co-occurrence data, hence there may exist the problem of topic drift [26].

6   Conclusion and Future Work

This work presents a method to recommend tags for mashups. Our proposed method employs attention mechanism in natural language processing (NLP), to learn the interactions between words in mashup description in order to reveal the functional properties in those descriptions. We first train a vector representation of words using web APIs and mashup descriptions. Then using this trained embeddings, we train an attention model to learn the interactions between the words in a mashup description. The attention model assigns weights to each word in the mashup description and highest weights are recommended as mashup tags. We have showed how our model is constructed, trained and discussed some results from our model.

While most of the results are encouraging, we will continue to tune our model and include more text from www.programmableweb.com in order to learn more embeddings of such words. These we plan to do as future work along with validating our model with current state-of-the-art methods.

References

1. Fletcher, K.K.: A quality-based web API selection for mashup development using affinity propagation. In: Ferreira, J.E., Spanoudakis, G., Ma, Y., Zhang, L.-J. (eds.) SCC 2018. LNCS, vol. 10969, pp. 153–165. Springer, Cham (2018). https://doi.org/10.1007/978-3-319-94376-3_10
2. Fletcher, K.: Regularizing matrix factorization with implicit user preference embeddings for web API recommendation. In: 2019 IEEE International Conference on Services Computing (SCC), pp. 1–8. IEEE (2019)
3. Santos, W.: Research Shows Interest in Providing APIs Still High. Accessed 18 Oct 2018
4. Shi, M., Liu, J., Zhou, D., Tang, Y.: A topic-sensitive method for mashup tag recommendation utilizing multi-relational service data. IEEE Trans. Serv. Comput. (2018)
5. Si, X., Sun, M.: Tag-LDA for scalable real-time tag recommendation. J. Inf. Comput. Sci. 6(2), 1009–1016 (2009)
6. Krestel, R., Fankhauser, P., Nejdl, W.: Latent Dirichlet allocation for tag recommendation. In: Proceedings of the Third ACM Conference on Recommender Systems, pp. 61–68. ACM (2009)
7. Fang, L., Wang, L., Li, M., Zhao, J., Zou, Y., Shao, L.: Towards automatic tagging for web services. In: 2012 IEEE 19th International Conference on Web Services, pp. 528–535. IEEE (2012)
8. Lin, M., Cheung, D.W.: Automatic tagging web services using machine learning techniques. In: Proceedings of the 2014 IEEE/WIC/ACM International Joint Conferences on Web Intelligence (WI) and Intelligent Agent Technologies (IAT), vol. 02, pp. 258–265. IEEE Computer Society (2014)
9. Kwapong, B.A., Anarfi, R., Fletcher, K.K.: Personalized service recommendation based on user dynamic preferences. In: Ferreira, J.E., Musaev, A., Zhang, L.-J. (eds.) SCC 2019. LNCS, vol. 11515, pp. 77–91. Springer, Cham (2019). https://doi.org/10.1007/978-3-030-23554-3_6

10. Yang, Z., Yang, D., Dyer, C., He, X., Smola, A., Hovy, E.: Hierarchical attention networks for document classification. In: Proceedings of the 2016 conference of the North American Chapter of the Association for Computational Linguistics: Human Language Technologies, pp. 1480–1489 (2016)

11. Pennington, J., Socher, R., Manning, C.D.: Glove: global vectors for word representation. In: Empirical Methods in Natural Language Processing (EMNLP), pp. 1532–1543 (2014)

12. Bahdanau, D., Cho, K., Bengio, Y.: Neural machine translation by jointly learning to align and translate. arXiv preprint arXiv:1409.0473 (2014)

13. Xu, K., et al.: Show, attend and tell: neural image caption generation with visual attention. In: International Conference on Machine Learning, pp. 2048–2057 (2015)

14. Gupta, S.: Word Embeddings in NLP and its Applications. Accessed 15 Nov 2019

15. Weng, L.: Attention? Attention! Accessed 15 Nov 2019

16. Fletcher, K.K.: A quality-aware web API recommender system for mashup development. In: Ferreira, J.E., Musaev, A., Zhang, L.-J. (eds.) SCC 2019. LNCS, vol. 11515, pp. 1–15. Springer, Cham (2019). https://doi.org/10.1007/978-3-030-23554-3_1

17. Shi, M., Liu, J., Zhou, D., Tang, M., Xie, F., Zhang, T.: A probabilistic topic model for mashup tag recommendation. In: 2016 IEEE International Conference on Web Services (ICWS), pp. 444–451, June 2016

18. Yin, Y., Zhao, Y., Zhang, B.: GDC: an efficient tag recommendation algorithm. In: 2015 12th International Conference on Fuzzy Systems and Knowledge Discovery (FSKD), pp. 1382–1387. IEEE (2015)

19. Zhou, P., Liu, J., Yang, Z., Zhou, G.: Scalable tag recommendation for software information sites. In: 2017 IEEE 24th International Conference on Software Analysis, Evolution and Reengineering (SANER), pp. 272–282. IEEE (2017)

20. Zhong, S., Lei, K., Huang, X., Wu, J.: Topic representation: a novel method of tag recommendation for text. In: 2017 IEEE 2nd International Conference on Big Data Analysis (ICBDA), pp. 671–676. IEEE (2017)

21. Belém, F., Martins, E., Almeida, J., Gonçalves, M.: Personalized and object-centered tag recommendation methods for web 2.0 applications. Inf. Process. Manag. **50**, 524–553 (2014)

22. Liu, Z., Chen, X., Sun, M.: A simple word trigger method for social tag suggestion. In: Proceedings of the Conference on Empirical Methods in Natural Language Processing. EMNLP 2011, Stroudsburg, PA, USA, pp. 1577–1588. Association for Computational Linguistics (2011)

23. Si, X., Sun, M.: Tag-LDA for scalable real-time tag recommendation. J. Comput. Inf. Syst. **6**, November 2008

24. Wang, H., Chen, B., Li, W.J.: Collaborative topic regression with social regularization for tag recommendation. In: Proceedings of the Twenty-Third International Joint Conference on Artificial Intelligence. IJCAI 2013, pp. 2719–2725. AAAI Press (2013)

25. Menezes, G.V., et al.: Demand-driven tag recommendation. In: Balcázar, J.L., Bonchi, F., Gionis, A., Sebag, M. (eds.) ECML PKDD 2010. LNCS (LNAI), vol. 6322, pp. 402–417. Springer, Heidelberg (2010). https://doi.org/10.1007/978-3-642-15883-4_26

26. Zhao, W., Guan, Z., Liu, Z.: Ranking on heterogeneous manifolds for tag recommendation in social tagging services. Neurocomputing **148**, 521–534 (2015)

Application Track

On the Diffusion and Impact of Code Smells in Web Applications

Narjes Bessghaier[1]([⊠]), Ali Ouni[1], and Mohamed Wiem Mkaouer[2]

[1] Ecole de Technologie Superieure (ETS), University of Quebec, Montreal, QC,
Canada
narjes.bessghaier.1@ens.etsmtl.ca, ali.ouni@etsmtl.ca
[2] Rochester Institute of Technology (RIT), Rochester, NY, USA
mwmvse@rit.edu

Abstract. Web applications (web apps) have become one of the largest
parts of the current software market over years. Modern web apps offer
several business benefits over other traditional and standalone applications. Mainly, cross-platform compatibility and data integration are some
of the critical features that encouraged businesses to shift towards the
adoption of Web apps. Web apps are evolving rapidly to acquire new
features, correct errors or adapt to new environment changes especially
with the volatile context of the web development. These ongoing amends
often affect software quality due to poor coding and bad design practices,
known as *code smells* or *anti-patterns*. The presence of code smells in a
software project is widely considered as form of technical debt and makes
the software harder to understand, maintain and evolve, besides leading
to failures and unforeseen costs. Therefore, it is critical for web apps to
monitor the existence and spread of such anti-patterns. In this paper,
we specifically target web apps built with PHP being the most used
server-side programming language. We conduct the first empirical study
to investigate the diffuseness of code smells in Web apps and their relationship with the change proneness of affected code. We detect 12 types
of common code smells across a total of 223 releases of 5 popular and
long-lived open-source web apps. The key findings of our study include:
1) complex and large classes and methods are frequently committed in
PHP files, 2) smelly files are more prone to change than non-smelly files,
and 3) *Too Many Methods* and *High Coupling* are the most associated
smells with files change-proneness.

Keywords: Code smells · Web applications · PHP · Diffuseness ·
Change proneness

1 Introduction

Web applications as defined by Google[1] are: *"...modern web capabilities to deliver
an app-like user experience..."*. Web apps are characterized by their inherent

---

[1] https://developers.google.com/web/updates/2015/12/getting-started-pwa.

© Springer Nature Switzerland AG 2020
Q. Wang et al. (Eds.): SCC 2020, LNCS 12409, pp. 67–84, 2020.
https://doi.org/10.1007/978-3-030-59592-0_5

heterogeneous nature in (1) target platforms as web apps are usually split in their client and server sides, and (2) formalisms as web apps are typically built with a mixture of programming and formatting languages. Such heterogeneity makes the evolution of web applications unique and different than traditional software systems.

Like any software application, web apps evolve rapidly to add new users functionalities, fix bugs, and adapt to new environmental changes. Such frequent and unavoidable changes, in the volatile context of the web development, can alter the quality of these applications. Indeed, acknowledged software design principles and practices are needed to be in place and empowered to support web apps development life-cycle. However, as software decays, some bad design and implementation practices may appear, which are known as *code smells* or *anti-patterns* [4,8]. Code smells are symptoms of poor design and implementation choices applied by developers that may hinder the comprehensibility and maintainability of software systems. Common code smells include, large classes, long methods, long parameter list, high coupling, complex class, etc. [4,8].

Several research efforts have been dedicated to studying code smells in traditional desktop software systems. It refers to bad coding practices that are committed mostly without the developers' knowledge [35]. Some studies focused on analyzing how code smells are introduced in the codebase [2,34,35], and how long they persist in the system [28,34]. Other studies focused on the impact of code smells on systems change and fault-proneness [21,32], and whether developers perceive these smells as problematic [2]. However, little is known about code smells diffuseness and impact for web applications. We cannot assume without empirical evidence the applicability of the prior findings on web apps as they widely differ. A dynamic web application package may encompass different technologies as JS, HTML, CSS, and PHP combining both programming and formatting aspects, which unlock another dimension of complexity, in comparison with traditional desktop applications. For example, web apps support combining code fragments, allowing to code PHP or JS inside HTML pages and vice versa. This coding practice emerges new types of code smells violating the *separation of concerns* design principle [30]. On a technical level, heterogeneous and dynamic web apps are more complex. Intensive computing tasks are performed to deal with databases and the HTTP client side's requests, which require more coding and maintenance efforts jeopardizing their quality and performance.

In this paper, we conduct the first empirical study on the diffuseness of code smells in web applications and investigate the impact of code smells on the source code change-proneness, *i.e.*, to investigate whether smelly files tend to require a higher frequency of changes when updating the files, as a side effect of their infection with bad programming practices. Moreover, we individually investigate how each smell type can contribute differently to the change-proneness. In particular, we focus our study on PHP-based web applications, being the top programming language used in server-side applications development. Indeed, nearly 79% of web apps are using PHP[2]. However, despite the popularity of the language in

---

[2] https://w3techs.com/technologies/overview/programming_language.

web development, no previous studies have empirically examined the behavior of code smells and how they impact the system's maintainability. To conduct our empirical study, we mined the historical changes of 223 releases from 5 popular web projects, phpMyAdmin, Joomla, WordPress, Piwik, and Laravel, to detect the existence of 12 common code smell types. The study provides empirical evidence that files containing code smells are more susceptible to change than non-smelly files, which negatively hinders the development of web apps, when containing code smells, as developers spend a larger amount of time and effort to update them. Results show that, at least, smelly-files are 2 times more prone to changes. Specifically, developers tend to write long and complex methods which make the code more hard to understand and modify. The obtained results indicate that the *High Method Complexity* and the *Excessive Method Length* code smells are frequently committed in PHP files. On the other hand, other smells such as the *Too Many Methods* and *High Coupling* are not frequently occurring, but they are the most smells leading to higher change-proneness. Findings from this study provide empirical evidence for practitioners that detecting and assessing code smells impact is of paramount importance to effectively reduce maintenance costs, as well as for the research community to concentrate their refactoring efforts on most harmful code smells. Further, this study serves as a first step to assess the magnitude of the severity of change-proneness related smells compared to other factors such as the number of occurrences of the smell and a class fault-proneness. We encourage the community to further harvest the data we collected by publishing our dataset for replication and extension purposes [1].

The rest of the paper is structured as follows. Section 2 presents the related literature on the diffuseness and impact of code smells. Section 3 describes the design of our empirical study. Section 4 presents and discusses the main findings. Threats to validity are discussed in Sect. 5. We conclude and highlight our main future research directions in Sect. 6.

2   Related Work

A number of studies exist on code smells in traditional software systems. We divide the existing works on 2 main categories (*i*) studies on the diffuseness and evolution of code smells, and (*ii*) studies on the impact of code smells.

2.1   Diffuseness and Evolution of Code Smells

There exists little knowledge of code smells in web applications. Recently, Rio et al. [31] targeted the survival probability of six code smell types using PHPMD[3], a PHP-based code smells detection tool, in 4 web applications. They considered three *scattered* smells (concern coupled entities) and three *localised* smells (concern an entity in itself). The findings did not show consistent behavior across the four systems. The survivability rate varies with the type of smells

---

[3] https://phpmd.org.

for each application. However, the introduction and removal events are higher in favor of *localised* smells. This can be explained by how code practices coupling several system components are harder to maintain. Nguyen et al. [19] proposed a detection tool *WebScent* of six kinds of the so-called embedded code smells that violate three design principles (*separation of concerns, software modularity, and compliance with coding standards*). The approach consisted of detecting code smells in the portions of PHP scripts responsible for generating the client-side code. The analysis highlighted that up to 81% of server files suffer from embedded code smells. Consequently, these files have a lower quality than smell-free files. Ouni et al. [22,24] introduced an automated approach to detect Web service anti-patterns in WSDL-based Web services.

However, to the best of our knowledge, no study has investigated the diffuseness of code smells in Web server-side projects and their relationship with development activities. Thus, we present the related literature on code smells in other programming languages. Palomba et al. [28] have investigated the diffuseness of code smells in desktop software systems and found that code smells related to large and complex code are most persistent in the system. They also investigated the correlation between the smell types and systems characteristics (*e.g.*, number of classes, number of methods, and lines of code LOC). Code smells are indeed diffused in large systems. Interestingly, this correlation does hold with smell types representing the more functional and sophisticated side of the system as like *Long method* and *complex class*. Olbrich et al. [20] analyzed the evolution of *God Class*, and *Shotgun Surgery* code smells in two open-source projects. The study first concluded that the evolution of smells is not steady along with the evolution of the systems. Concerning the change-proneness, they highlighted that smelly files exhibit more change. Same results are witnessed when considering the *God Class*, and *Brain Class* in the evolution of three projects [21]. The study consisted of analyzing the impact of smells on the change frequency (number of commits in which a file has changed) and change size (code churn) of files. An important conclusion highlighted that classes containing the examined smells are more prone to change frequency and change size. However, when the *God* and *Brain* classes are normalized with respect to size (per LOC), they are less subject to change. In the same line, Chatzigeorgiou et al. [5] studied the evolution of *Long method, Feature Envy*, and *State Checking* code smells in 24 releases of two Java projects (JFlex, and JFreeChart). In all examined releases, the *Long Method*, which signifies a large-sized piece of code, had exponential growth as a system evolves. Contrary to the *Feature Envy* and *State Checking*, which have shown a steady low rate of evolution.

2.2   Relationship Between Code Smells and Development Activities

Khomh et al. [12] conducted an empirical analysis on 13 different releases of Azureus and Eclipse, considering 9 code smells, to investigate three relationships. (*i*) smelly classes are more exposed to frequent updates than others (3 to 8 times in favor of smelly classes). (*ii*) the more a class has instances of smells, the more it is change-prone. (*iii*) particular but not common kinds of smells lead to more change-proneness than others. An extended study examined code smells impact in 54 releases of four projects [13] confirmed that smelly classes are more subject to change and faults. These results were confirmed by Spadini et al. [33], who found that the presence of test smells yields to more code changes, which might produce bugs in the production code. Saboury et al. [32] have carried out an empirical investigation on the impact of 12 JavaScript code smells on the fault-proneness of modified classes of five projects. They compared the fault-proneness between smelly and non-smelly files using the survival analysis test to capture a longitudinal behavior. The results show that non-smelly files have a 65% chance less than files with smells. As well, they opted for a Cox Hazard test to asses the impact of three factors on the survivability of faults (LOC, Code churn, and the number of Previous Bugs). Their results indicate that the number of Previous-Bugs, which means the number of fault-fixing changes, is fault-inducing. Aniche et al. [2] examined when code smells are introduced and how long they survive using the survival analysis test. Their study highlighted some important points (*i*) code smells are more introduced from the first release of the system, and (*ii*) code smells that are present with the first commits tend to survive more.

3   Empirical Study Design

As presented in Fig. 1, our empirical study aims at analyzing the *diffuseness* and *impact* of code smells in web applications. The diffuseness refers to the rate of code smells in code components (classes, methods), *i.e.*, how many parts of the application are affected by at least one instance of code smells. The analysis of smells distribution helps to better assess (1) the impact of code smells on the change-proneness of smelly files, and (2) how specific code smell types could result into different change sizes. It is worth noting that some smell types could lead to more change-proneness but are poorly diffused and vise versa.

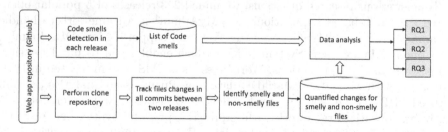

Fig. 1. Overview of our empirical study.

To collect our dataset for our empirical study, we considered a set of common code smell types in Web software applications. To detect instance of code smells in our benchmark, we use PHPMD [29], a widely used tool for quality assurance and code smells detection specialized for PHP software applications. We considered a list of 12 smell types as they are most known, and widely being discussed in recent studies [7,9,15,16,31]. It is worth noting that we selected class-level and method-level code smells that affect the source code's understandability or might aggravate the performance to capture a broad analysis of our studied phenomena. Although, PHPMD supports the detection of 36 types of design flaws, we basically considered common code smell types [3,18,23,25–27,31] and excluded smells related to low level violations such as calling the `var_dump()` function in the production code. Table 1 provides the list of the considered code smells along with their definitions.

3.1 Research Questions

We formulate the following research questions.

- **RQ1:** *What is the diffuseness of code smells in web apps?* We aim to know the most diffused and frequently occurring code smells to recognize which bad coding practices are more common and thus prioritize their refactoring.
- **RQ2:** *To what extent files affected by code smells exhibit a different level of change-proneness as compared to non-smelly files?* We aim to assess whether smelly files undergo more maintenance activities compared to non-smelly files by testing the following null hypotheses:
  $H2_0$: Smelly files are not more prone to change during the software evolution as compared to non-smelly files.
- **RQ3:** *What is the relationship between specific types of code smells and the level of change-proneness?* We investigate whether some smell types contribute more to the change-proneness of smelly classes. To answer our research question, we test the validity of the following null hypothesis.
  $H3_0$: Smelly files undergo the same level of change-proneness for all smell types.

To answer our research questions, we mined 223 releases of 5 popular open-source PHP web-based applications. PhpMyAdmin[4] is a framework to handle the administration of MySQL over the Web and supports MariaDB. Joomla[5] is a Content Management System (CMS) which enables you to build websites and powerful online applications. WordPress[6] is a CMS system written in PHP and paired with MySQL or MariaDB database. Piwik[7] is an analytics and full featured PHP MySQL software to download and install on webserver. Laravel[8] is a web application framework with expressive, powerful syntax and provides tools required for large, robust applications. We chose applications with different sizes ranging from 12 to 662 KLOCs. As presented in Table 2, the studied

---

[4] https://github.com/phpmyadmin/phpmyadmin.
[5] https://github.com/joomla/joomla-cms.
[6] https://github.com/WordPress/WordPress.
[7] https://github.com/matomo-org/matomo.
[8] https://github.com/laravel/laravel.

Table 1. List of code smells considered in our study

Code smell	Description
Excessive Number Of Children (ENOC)	A class with too many descendants usually indicates an unbalanced class hierarchy [29, 31]
Excessive Depth Of Inheritance (EDOI)	A class with a deep inheritance tree can lead to an unmaintainable code as the coupling would increase [29, 31]
High Coupling (HC)	A class with too many dependencies makes it harder to maintain and evolve [8, 16, 29, 31]
Empty Catch Block (ECB)	Fixing an execution failure of an unknown exception type will require more efforts to understand the error condition [29]
Goto Statement (GTS)	Goto makes the logic of an application hard to understand [29]
High Method Complexity (HMC)	The cyclomatic complexity at the method level represents the number of decision points (e.g., if, for, while). The higher the number of decision points, the higher the number of test cases needed to test all the different execution paths [9, 29]
High NPath Complexity (HNPC)	The NPath complexity is the number of ways (nested if/else statements) the code can get executed, which would decrease the readability of the code and cause testing issues [29]
Excessive Method Length (EML)	When a method exceeds 100 NCLOC, it is considered a broad method that does too much. These methods are likely to end up processing data differently than what their context suggests until they become hard to understand and maintain [7, 9, 16, 29, 31]
Excessive Class Length (ECL)	Large classes are a good suspect for refactoring, as their size represents a challenge to manage efficiently, and maintain them [15, 16, 29, 31]
Excessive Parameter List (EPL)	A long parameter set can indicate that a method is doing too many different things, which makes it harder to understand its behavior [7, 17, 29, 31]
Too Many Public Methods (TMPM)	A large number of public methods indicate that the class does not preserve its data encapsulated. Consequently, changing the internal behavior of the class requires additional efforts not to risk damaging some dependencies. In practice, we cannot restrict the number of public methods. Only what could be exposed should be public. If external classes are extensively accessing these methods, they should be moved to reduce the coupling [29]
Too Many Methods (TMM)	The Too Many Methods is the symptom of a class that contains a large number of methods that typically do not belong to its responsibilities and consequently decreases the cohesion level [29]

projects belong to different application domains and actively engineered during 9 to 15 years. Table 2 reports the number of considered releases, the number of stars on Github, and we count the applications size in terms of the number of classes, methods, and KLOCs for each project using the PHPLOC tool[9].

Table 2. The studied systems statistics.

Name	Releases	Period	Stars	# classes	KLOCs	# smells
phpMyAdmin	55	2014–2020	4.7k	30–645	228–328	60,695
Joomla	34	2011–2019	3.4k	1,102–2,631	271–662	75,616
WordPress	74	2005–2019	13.4k	24–496	37–391	106,962
Piwik	38	2010–2020	12.6k	1,017–2,095	242–374	39,896
Laravel	22	2012–2020	57.3k	95–248	12–40	1,647

3.2   Analysis Method

To answer **RQ1**, we first compute the absolute number of code smells present in each application (aggregation of releases). Then, we assess the number of affected classes for each smell type. To better position the number of smells with respect to the size of the application, we assess the diffuseness of smells per KLOC.

To answer **RQ2**, we use the git versioning system to mine the change history of the five applications. We identify all modified PHP files in each commit between the releases r_{j-1} and r_j. Then, we extract the number of modification each modified file has undergone using the following git command:
`$ git show --stat --no-commit-id --oneline -r SHA1..SHA2"*.php"`
Then, we identify the nature of the returned modified files whether it is a *smelly* or a *non-smelly* class. Thereafter, we compute the change-proneness of a modified class c as the sum of the changes performed in all commits between the releases r_{j-1} and r_j.

$$Change\text{-}proneness(c, r_j) = \sum_{i=1}^{i=n} churn(c, com_i) \tag{1}$$

where n is the number of commits between releases r_{j-1} and r_j, the function $churn(c, com_i)$ returns the code churn in terms of number of added, removed and modified lines of code in the class c in commit com_i using the GitHub API[10]. After the extraction of all data, we compare the change-proneness of smelly and non-smelly classes using the beanplot representation [11]. A beanplot extends the boxplot's visualization by representing the density of data distribution along with the individual observations. To assess $H2_0$, we verify whether

---

[9] https://github.com/sebastianbergmann/phploc.
[10] https://developer.github.com/v3/.

there is a significant difference between the two tested populations (smelly, non-smelly). Therefore, after the data normality check (*p-value* = 0.8 and *p-value* = 0.6), we apply the parametric independent t-test [14] to check the magnitude of difference between our two groups. The t-test serves to evaluate the alternative hypothesis stating how likely one sample exhibits dominance compared with the other sample. We consolidate the test by measuring the parametric Cohen-d effect size. As stated by [6], the effect size tells how important the difference between the two samples is. An effect size is considered small if $0.2 \leq d < 0.5$, medium if $0.5 \leq d < 0.8$ and large if $d \geq 0.8$. It is worth noting that we consider a class as smelly only if it has at least one instance of code smell. We narrowed the gap between smelly and non-smelly classes to deeply analyze the phenomenon of change-proneness considering most harmful smells. Moreover, if a class changes from smelly to non-smelly in some releases and vise versa, it contributes to both sets of smelly and non-smelly classes.

To answer **RQ3**, we assess the impact of smells types on the change-proneness. We compute the number of occurrences of each smell type in the smelly classes of each release. We quantify the impact of each smell type for each project as the correlation score between the sum of the frequency count of each smell type ST_i and the class state {0 or 1} representing whether a class has changed or not between two releases $r_{j-1} \rightarrow r_j$. To statistically analyze the effect of each smell type on a class change-proneness, we opted for a *logistic regression* test [10] similar to khomh et al. [12] to reject the null hypothesis $H3_0$ stating that classes undergo the same change size for all types of smells. The logistic regression should decide whether the class would change for each smell type. To asses the change of a class based on a set of smells, a class would represent the dependent variable C_i that would change if one of the smell types ST_j (independent variable) changes as well. In a logistic model, the dependent variable could take only two values (changed = 1, not changed = 0). Thus, our multivariate model equation applied to a class C_i in a release r_t is defined as follows:

$$P(C_i) = \frac{e(CP + \sum_1^{12} b_j * ST_j)}{1 + e(CP + \sum_1^{12} b_j * ST_j)} \quad \in [0,1] \tag{2}$$

where P is the likelihood that a class changes; CP is the change proneness of a class {0,1}; and b_j is the number of occurrences of a smell type ST_j.

We apply our logistic regression model for each smell type detected in the 223 releases in our benchmark. Then, we count the number of times the *p-value* of a smell is significant (the probability is closer to 1).

4 Study Results and Analysis

4.1 RQ1: Code Smells Diffuseness

Figure 2 reports (*i*) the absolute number of code smells distribution in the analyzed projects, (*ii*) the number of affected classes by each code smell type, and (*iii*) the density of code smells per KLOCs using the beanplot visualization. For the sake of clarity, we aggregate the occurrences of each code smell in our studied projects into one single dataset. From the beanplots and Table 3, we observe the existence of three main categories of code smell distributions (1) highly diffused and highly frequent, (2) highly diffused and slightly frequent, and (3) slightly diffused and slightly frequent.

Highly Diffused and Highly Frequent Smells: As shown in Fig. 2 and Table 3, the *High Method Complexity* smell is the most diffused (99%) and frequent (42%) code smell. It typically manifests in the form of a high cyclomatic complexity level within the methods. We found that this smell has a high number of occurrences with 1,250 instances in the two last studied releases of `Joomla` (3.9.13 and 3.9.14). For instance, the class `Joomla.CMS.Form.Form` in release 3.9.13 has a cyclomatic complexity of 64 in its method `filterField()` responsible for applying an input filter to a value based on field data. These methods are in general very long (on average, 261 LOC found in *Joomla* studied releases). Moreover, we found that the *High NPath Complexity* occurs also in 99% of the releases, representing 27% of the total number of detected smells. It has a total of 820 occurrences in `Joomla` 3.9.13. Alike, *Excessive Method Length* impacts 95% of the releases, representing 16% of the smells with a peak reaching 556 in `WordPress` 5.3.2. Indeed, we found 12 long methods using AJAX with an average of 143 LOC. Moreover, from a qualitative sense, the diffuseness of smell instances per KLOC is reported in Fig. 2c which confirms that the *High Method Complexity*, the *High NPath Complexity*, and the *Excessive Method Length* are the most diffused smells with an average of 24, 17, and 13 instances respectively.

Highly Diffused and Slightly Frequent Smells: This category of smells occur in the majority of the studied releases but with a limited number of instances. As shown in Fig. 2 and Table 3, we observe that the *High Coupling* smell exists in 98% of the releases, but representing only 2% of the accumulated number of smells. For instance, we found that the *High Coupling* smell reaches the bar of 99 instances in both releases of `Piwik` 3.13.0 and 3.13.1. On average, each of the infected releases has 25 instances of this smell. As compared to other studies in Android apps, the *High Coupling* is found to have weak diffuseness and frequency as pointed by Mannan et al. [16]. To better understand this disparity in terms of diffuseness, we conducted a closer analysis on the 3.13.0 release of `Piwik`. Most of the instances are located in the `Archive`, and `ArchiveProcessor` packages. In particular, the class `CronArchive` in `Archive` package has a coupling between objects (CBO) score of 33 surpassing the established threshold of 13 which is considered as normal [29]. Hence, this disparity in the diffuseness rate of the *High Coupling* between Android and web apps could be related to the small size of Android apps along with their different structure and workflow which typically come with a low coupling between code components.

Moreover, we found that the *Excessive Class Length*, the *Too Many Public Methods*, the *Excessive Number Of Children*, and the *Too Many Methods* are not frequent as they have a maximum number of occurrences per class that do not exceed 5. For example, the *Too Many Public Methods* smell represents 5% of the total number of smells, and is distributed across 86% of the releases as shown in Fig. 2 and Table 3. Most diffused instances are in Joomla with a high number of occurrences of 234 in the last five releases (from v3.9.7 to v3.9.14). Likewise, among the highly diffused, but slightly frequent code smells, we found the *Too Many Public Methods* smell which have more instances per KLOC (6). In addition, the *Empty Catch Block* and *Excessive Parameter List* code smells are impacting 65% and 89% of releases with the highest number of occurrences of 69 in Piwik (2.17.1 and 2.18.0) and 40 in Piwik 2.12.1 respectively. The *Excessive Parameter List* has the highest occurrence number (19) of all slightly frequent smells in the method image() in the package com.tecnick.tcpdf. The *Excessive Parameter List* is a one single-metric violation that straightforwardly detects the smell. Besides, it is also worth noting that, Wordpress and phpMyAdmin applications have no instance of the *Empty Catch Block*, which is limited to one instance per KLOC.

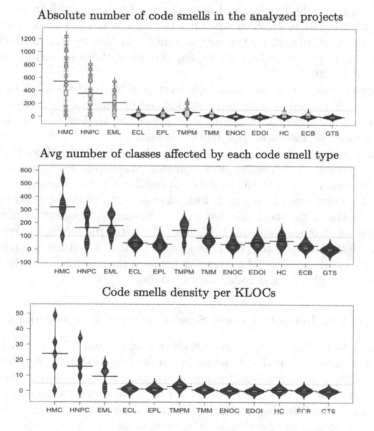

Fig. 2. The absolute number, % affected classes, and density per KLOC of smells.

Slightly Diffused and Slightly Frequent Smells: As shown in Fig. 2 and Table 3, the *Excessive Depth Of Inheritance* and the *Go to Statement* code smells are slightly diffused and not frequent. Overall, the *Excessive Depth Of Inheritance* smell exists only in 20 classes, impacting only 4% of the studied releases, and it represents nearly 1% of the total number of detected code smells. For instance, we found that the highest number of occurrences of the *Excessive Depth Of Inheritance* smell is 10 in `Piwik` 1.8.0. Similarly, the *Goto Statement* smell represents nearly 1% of the total number of code smells and affects 2% of the studied releases. This particular smell occurs only in `phpMyAdmin` (10% of the releases of phpMyAdmin), with a negligible percentage of ~1% of the total number of code smells detected in `phpMyAdmin`. Since its spread is limited to a few classes, the correction of *Goto Statement* becomes easier for developers.

Table 3 reports the diffuseness of code smells according to the accumulated number of releases. The "% of affected releases" column represents the percentage of affected releases by a particular smell. For example, the *Too Many Methods* smell impacts 77% of the releases. The "max instances" column reports the highest number of occurrences of a given smell in a class. For instance, the *Too Many Methods* smell has the highest number of occurrences in the `libraries.simplepi.e.simplepi.e.php` file in Joomla `2.5.3` which has 5 classes having respectively 102, 40, 40, 35, and 26 methods exceeding the basic threshold of 25 [29].

To sum up, most of the smells are quite diffused in the studied subjects. Particularly, smells related to long and complex code fragments (*i.e.*, *High Method Complexity*, *High NPath Complexity*, and *Excessive Method Length*) have the highest number of instances per KLOC, and impact the highest number of classes. Our findings align with those of Palomba et al. [28] on Java traditional code smells, where *Long method* and *Complex Class* code smells are the most diffused. Moreover, 3/4 of the analyzed code smells are not frequent (*i.e.*, limited number of occurrences per release), but affecting 68% of the studied projects. Besides, `Joomla` is the most affected project having the maximum number of occurrences of four smells *High Method Complexity*, *High NPath Complexity*, *Excessive Method Length*, and *Too Many Public method*. By studying code smells diffuseness, we aim to assess the interplay between the magnitude of the diffuseness for each smell type and code maintainability.

4.2   RQ2: The Impact of Code Smells on the Change-Proneness

The beanplots in Fig. 3 illustrate the change size range of both smelly and non-smelly classes. As previously found in studies targeting Java object-oriented systems [13, 28], code smells lead to more code changes in a class and thus require higher maintenance efforts. As reported in Fig. 3, we witnessed similar findings, as we found that smelly classes clearly exhibit a higher level of change-proneness as compared to non-smelly classes. The median of change-proneness (CP) of smelly classes is 12.8 which is almost three times higher than the non-smelly classes (4.1). For example, the median change in `Laravel` is 2 against a median of 4 in the smelly classes. The intense density shape in the non-smelly class set demonstrates how the majority of non-smelly classes experience similar change

Table 3. Diffuseness of code smells in the analyzed projects

Code smell	% affected releases	% of smells	Max instances
High Method Complexity	99%	42%	96
High NPath Complexity	99%	27%	76
Excessive Method Length	95%	16%	42
High Coupling	98%	2%	2
Excessive Class Length	98%	2%	3
Excessive Parameter List	89%	1%	19
Too Many Public Methods	86%	5%	5
Excessive Number of Children	78%	~1%	1
Too Many Methods	77%	1%	5
Goto Statement	2%	~1%	1
Empty Catch Block	65%	1%	4
Excessive Depth of Inheritance	4%	~1%	1

rate. For instance, 41 non-smelly classes in `Laravel` that are responsible for languages setting underwent almost the same modifications size. Unlike the smelly-classes, each has its maintenance requirements, which seems to be related to the co-existence of different types of code smells such as *High Method Complexity* and *Excessive Method Length*. Referring to statistical evidence, the t-test shows a statistically significant difference with a *p-value* = 0.03, while Cohen *d* shows a large effect size of 1.8, allowing us to reject the null hypothesis $H2_0$. To sum up, the majority of releases are affected by smells. However, the large portion of the modified classes in each project are smells-free. Still, smelly classes undergo more changes, and thus, exhibiting a higher level of change-proneness than non smelly classes.

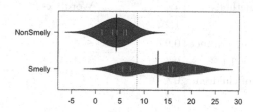

Fig. 3. Change-proneness of smelly and non-smelly classes.

4.3 RQ3: The Impact of Code Smells Types on the Change-Proneness

Table 4 reports the results of the logistic regression model for RQ3. The reported values refer to the percentage of releases for which the correspondent smell type is statistically significant in the logistic model with a $p-value < 0.05$. We observe that the existence of smells does impact the majority of projects in terms of increasing the proneness of their infected files, and this impact varies from one project to another. More precisely, we highlight the *High Method Complexity (HMC)*, *Excessive Method Length (EML)* and *Too Many Methods (TMM)* smell types, as they exhibit the highest impact on the change-proneness on 32%, 28% and 25% of the releases, respectively. In particular, HMC has shown an impact on two out of the five projects, namely *Piwik* and *WordPress*, and EML has an impact on *phpMyAdmin* and *Laravel*, while TMM impacted 3 projects (*Joomla, Laravel* and *phpMyAdmin*). On the other side, we observe that other smells such as the *Excessive Parameter List*, the *Excessive Number of Children*, and *Goto Statement* do not have statistically significant impact on the change-proneness on any release or project. This can be due to the fact that the latter smells are found to be slightly diffused and slightly frequent, as observed in RQ1.

Table 4. The results of the logistic regression model reporting the number of releases and projects for which each smell type is statistically significant.

Code smell	% sig. releases	Projects
High method complexity	32%	Piwik, WordPress
Excessive method length	28%	phpMyAdmin, Laravel
Too many methods	25%	Joomla, Laravel, phpMyAdmin
High coupling	21%	Piwik, WordPress, phpMyAdmin
Excessive class length	13%	phpMyadmin, Laravel
High NPath complexity	12%	Piwik
Too many public methods	4%	WordPress
Empty catch block	1.2%	–
Excessive depth of inheritance	0.9%	–
Excessive parameter list	0%	–
Excessive number of children	0%	–
Goto statement	0%	–

The main insights that we can draw from these findings could be summarized as follows (1) the slightly diffused and slightly frequent code smells have no statistically significant impact on change-proneness of files across the five projects. Hence, not all smells should be given equal removal priority. For instance, the *GoTo Statement* and *Excessive Depth Of Inheritance* are not seen as problematic, as they do not cause an increase in the number of code changes; (2) Classes in *Joomla* tend to experience an increase on change percentage whenever there is a variation in the number of *Too Many Methods* instances. (3) diffuseness and frequency of smells do not necessarily correlate with their ability to impact change-proneness of files. For example, The *High method Complexity* smell has shown the highest diffuseness in 99% of the releases (cf. Table 3), yet, its statistically significant impact on files change-proneness is limited to only two projects.

We can conclude that the impact of smells varies by type and by project. Existence of smells is alarming since they increase the chance of experiencing higher change rate, especially with *Too Many Methods* and *High Coupling* that scored the highest impact in our experiment. Since for each project, at least one single smell is showing an effect on the change-proneness. Thus, we reject the null hypothesis $H3_0$. knowing the types of code smells leading to more change-proneness will aid in preparing specific refactoring plans and focus on fixing the most harmful design and implementation practices.

5 Threats to Validity

The *Construct validity* concerns errors in measurements. In our context, we relied on the git versioning systems of each project to count the number of changes. For each release, we were interested in quantifying the changes in modified files. Moreover, while we considered 12 common code smells based on recent studies [18,31], there could be other code smell types to be considered. Moreover, similar to Khomh et al. [12], we used the logistic regression test to determine which smells are significant with the change-proneness.

The *Internal validity* concerns the factors that can limit the applicability of our observations. We assessed the cause-effect relation between the presence of code smells and the change-proneness of a file as the probability of smell to exert an impact on the state of a class. Still, we cannot assume that the changes made on a file are the result of code smells refactoring activities. Other improvement activities (exp. adding new functionalities) could yield to these changes. However, we expect that classes with high change-proneness represent the business logic of the system that does too much and gets frequently modified. Thus, these classes are more prone to having code smells and possibly exhibit more refactoring operations.

The *External validity* concerns the generalizability of our findings. We have analyzed a total of 5 PHP Web projects with different communities, sizes, and application domains and with a minimum of 9 years of history. We are aware that we cannot generalize our finding to other projects. In the future, we plan to reduce this threat further by analyzing more projects from more industrial and open-source software projects and other web programming languages.

6 Conclusion

This paper reported a large study conducted on 223 releases of five popular web-based applications. The empirical study aimed at understanding the diffuseness of code smells in web open source apps and their relation with source code change-proneness. The statistical analysis of the obtained results show that most diffused and frequent code smells are related to the size and complexity of code fragments. Moreover, our findings indicate that classes with such smells are more prone to change than other classes which may require more maintenance efforts. To provide better insights, we individually investigated the relationship between each smell type and the change-proneness using a logistic regression model. Results showed that specific smells do have an impact on the change-proneness of a class. However, the type of these change-inducing smells tend to be context related. Our findings indicate that *code smells should be carefully monitored by web programmers*, since they are diffused in web applications and related to maintainability aspects such as change-proneness. As future work, we first plan to replicate our study on other open source and industrial web applications. We plan also to analyze the impact of the co-occurences of code smells on the change-proneness. Moreover, we plan to investigate the impact of smelly-files on the fault-proneness. More interestingly, we will develop automated code smells refactoring recommendation and prioritization techniques in the context of web apps to better monitor code smells.

References

1. Replication package. https://github.com/Narjes-b/SmellsAnalysis-WebApps
2. Aniche, M., Bavota, G., Treude, C., Gerosa, M.A., van Deursen, A.: Code smells for model-view-controller architectures. Empirical Soft. Eng. **23**(4), 2121–2157 (2018)
3. Boukharata, S., Ouni, A., Kessentini, M., Bouktif, S., Wang, H.: Improving web service interfaces modularity using multi-objective optimization. Autom. Sofw. Eng. **26**(2), 275–312 (2019)
4. Brown, W.H., Malveau, R.C., McCormick, H.W., Mowbray, T.J.: AntiPatterns: Refactoring Software, Architectures, and Projects In Crisis. Wiley, New York (1998)
5. Chatzigeorgiou, A., Manakos, A.: Investigating the evolution of bad smells in object-oriented code. In: Seventh International Conference on the Quality of Information and Communications Technology, pp. 106–115. IEEE (2010)
6. Cohen, J.: Statistical Power Analysis for The Behavioral Sciences. Erihaum, Hillsdale (1988)
7. Delchev, M., Harun, M.F.: Investigation of code smells in different software domains. Full-scale Softw. Eng. **31**, 31–36 (2015)
8. Fowler, M.: Refactoring: Improving the Design of Existing Code. Addison-Wesley Professional, Boston (2018)
9. Hecht, G., Benomar, O., Rouvoy, R., Moha, N., Duchien, L.: Tracking the software quality of android applications along their evolution (t). In: International Conference on Automated Software Engineering (ASE), pp. 236–247 (2015)
10. Hosmer, D.W., Lemeshow, S., Cook, E.: Applied Logistic Regression, 2nd edn. Wiley, New York (2000)
11. Kampstra, P., et al.: Beanplot: a boxplot alternative for visual comparison of distributions. J. Stat. Softw. **28**(1), 1–9 (2008)
12. Khomh, F., Di Penta, M., Gueheneuc, Y.G.: An exploratory study of the impact of code smells on software change-proneness. In: WCRE, pp. 75–84 (2009)

13. Khomh, F., Di Penta, M., Guéhéneuc, Y.G., Antoniol, G.: An exploratory study of the impact of antipatterns on class change-and fault-proneness. Empirical Softw. Eng. **17**(3), 243–275 (2012). https://doi.org/10.1007/s10664-011-9171-y
14. Kim, T.K.: T test as a parametric statistic. Korean J. Anesthesiol. **68**(6), 540 (2015)
15. Liu, X., Zhang, C.: The detection of code smell on software development: a mapping study. In: 5th International Conference on Machinery, Materials and Computing Technology (ICMMCT 2017). Atlantis Press (2017)
16. Mannan, U.A., Ahmed, I., Almurshed, R.A.M., Dig, D., Jensen, C.: Understanding code smells in android applications. In: IEEE/ACM International Conference on Mobile Software Engineering and Systems (MOBILESoft), pp. 225–236 (2016)
17. Martin, R.C.: Clean Code: A Handbook of Agile Software Craftsmanship. Pearson Education, London (2009)
18. Mon, C.T., Hlaing, S., Tin, M., Khin, M., Lwin, T.M., Myo, K.M.: Code readability metric for PHP. In: IEEE 8th Global Conference on Consumer Electronics (GCCE), pp. 929–930 (2019)
19. Nguyen, H.V., Nguyen, H.A., Nguyen, T.T., Nguyen, A.T., Nguyen, T.N.: Detection of embedded code smells in dynamic web applications. In: IEEE/ACM International Conference on Automated Software Engineering, pp. 282–285 (2012)
20. Olbrich, S., Cruzes, D.S., Basili, V., Zazworka, N.: The evolution and impact of code smells: a case study of two open source systems. In: International Symposium on Empirical Software Engineering and Measurement, pp. 390–400 (2009)
21. Olbrich, S.M., Cruzes, D.S., Sjøberg, D.I.: Are all code smells harmful? A study of god classes and brain classes in the evolution of three open source systems. In: International Conference on Software Maintenance, pp. 1–10 (2010)
22. Ouni, A., Gaikovina Kula, R., Kessentini, M., Inoue, K.: Web service antipatterns detection using genetic programming. In: Annual Conference on Genetic and Evolutionary Computation (GECCO), pp. 1351–1358 (2015)
23. Ouni, A., Kessentini, M., Bechikh, S., Sahraoui, H.: Prioritizing code-smells correction tasks using chemical reaction optimization. Softw. Qual. J. **23**(2), 323–361 (2015)
24. Ouni, A., Kessentini, M., Inoue, K., Cinnéide, M.O.: Search-based web service antipatterns detection. IEEE Trans. Serv. Comput. **10**(4), 603–617 (2017)
25. Ouni, A., Kessentini, M., Ó cinnéide, M., Sahraoui, H., Deb, K., Inoue, K.: MORE: a multi-objective refactoring recommendation approach to introducing design patterns and fixing code smells. Softw. Evol. Process **29**(5), e1843 (2017)
26. Ouni, A., Kessentini, M., Sahraoui, H., Inoue, K., Deb, K.: Multi-criteria code refactoring using search-based software engineering: an industrial case study. ACM Trans. Softw. Eng. Methodol. **25**(3), 1–53 (2016)
27. Ouni, A., Kessentini, M., Sahraoui, H., Inoue, K., Hamdi, M.S.: Improving multi-objective code-smells correction using development history. J. Syst. Softw. **105**, 18–39 (2015)
28. Palomba, F., Bavota, G., Di Penta, M., Fasano, F., Oliveto, R., De Lucia, A.: On the diffuseness and the impact on maintainability of code smells: a large scale empirical investigation. Empirical Softw. Eng. **23**(3), 1188–1221 (2018). https://doi.org/10.1007/s10664-017-9535-z
29. PHPMD (2020). https://phpmd.org
30. Pressman, R.S.: Software engineering: a practitioner's approach. Palgrave Macmillan, London (2005)

31. Rio, A., Brito e Abreu, F.: Code smells survival analysis in web apps. In: Piattini, M., Rupino da Cunha, P., García Rodríguez de Guzmán, I., Pérez-Castillo, R. (eds.) QUATIC 2019. CCIS, vol. 1010, pp. 263–271. Springer, Cham (2019). https://doi.org/10.1007/978-3-030-29238-6_19
32. Saboury, A., Musavi, P., Khomh, F., Antoniol, G.: An empirical study of code smells in Javascript projects. In: International Conference on Software Analysis, Evolution and Reengineering, pp. 294–305 (2017)
33. Spadini, D., Palomba, F., Zaidman, A., Bruntink, M., Bacchelli, A.: On the relation of test smells to software code quality. In: IEEE International Conference on Software Maintenance and Evolution (ICSME), pp. 1–12. IEEE (2018)
34. Tufano, M., et al.: An empirical investigation into the nature of test smells. In: International Conference on Automated Software Engineering, pp. 4–15 (2016)
35. Tufano, M., et al.: When and why your code starts to smell bad. In: IEEE International Conference on Software Engineering, vol. 1, pp. 403–414 (2015)

Microservices Backlog - A Model of Granularity Specification and Microservice Identification

Fredy H. Vera-Rivera[1,2,4(✉)] ⓘ, Eduard G. Puerto-Cuadros[1] ⓘ,
Hernán Astudillo[3] ⓘ, and Carlos Mauricio Gaona-Cuevas[4]

[1] Universidad Francisco de Paula Santander, San José de Cúcuta, Colombia
fredyhumbertovera@ufps.edu.co
[2] Foundation of Researchers in Science and Technology of Materials,
Bucaramanga, Colombia
[3] Universidad Técnica Federico Santa María, Valparaíso, Chile
[4] Universidad del Valle, Cali, Colombia

Abstract. Microservices are a software development approach where applications are composed of small independent services that communicate through well-defined APIs. A major challenge of designing these applications is determining the appropriate microservices granularity, which is currently done by architects using their judgment. This article describes Microservice Backlog (MB), a fully automatic genetic-programming technique that uses the product backlog's user stories to (1) propose a set of microservices for optimal granularity and (2) allow architects to visualize at design time their design metrics. Also, a new Granularity Metric (GM) was defined that combines existing metrics of coupling, cohesion, and associated user stories. The MB-proposed decomposition for a well-known state-of-the-art case study was compared with three existing methods (two automatics and one semi-automatic); it had consistently better GM scoring and fewer average calls among microservices, and it allowed to identify critical points. The wider availability of techniques like MB will allow architects to automate microservices identification, optimize their granularity, visually assess their design metrics, and identify at design time the system critical points.

Keywords: Microservices architecture · Granularity · Decomposition · Cohesion metrics · Coupling metrics · Complexity metrics · User stories

1 Introduction

The microservices architectural changes the way applications are created, tested, implemented, and maintained. By using microservices, a large application can be implemented as a set of small applications that can be developed, deployed, expanded, managed, and monitored independently. Agility, cost reduction and granular scalability entail some challenges such as the complexity of managing distributed systems [1]. The appropriate size (granularity) of the microservice is one of their most discussed properties and there are few patterns, methods, or models to determine how small a

© Springer Nature Switzerland AG 2020
Q. Wang et al. (Eds.): SCC 2020, LNCS 12409, pp. 85–102, 2020.
https://doi.org/10.1007/978-3-030-59592-0_6

microservice should be. Thus Soldani et al. [2] argue that there is difficulty identifying the business capacities and delimited contexts that can be assigned to each microservice. Bogner et al. [3] note that methodologies and techniques must facilitate dimensioning and versioning of microservices. Zimmerman [4] wonders how to find an adequate service cut, (i.e. "how small or fine is small enough"). Jamshidi et al. [5] notice the lack of agreement on the correct size of microservices.

We introduce the Microservice Backlog, which allows to analyze graphically microservices granularity, starting from a set of functional requirements expressed as user stories within a product backlog (prioritized and characterized list of functionalities that an application must contain [6]); we propose a model that helps to define the size and number of microservices using genetic programming; it shows the microservices that are going to be part of an application detailing its dependencies, functionalities and coupling, cohesion, and complexity metrics at design time. Therefore, we can observe and evaluate the microservices' granularity and analyze how the application will be implemented and structured.

The major contributions from this work are: 1) a model for determining and evaluating the granularity of microservices, establishing the number of user stories assigned to a microservice and the number of microservices that are part of the application, ensuring that microservices have low coupling and high cohesion, 2) identified and adapted metrics of complexity, coupling, cohesion, and size of the microservice, 3) mathematical formalization of an application based on microservices in terms of user stories and metrics, and 4) A genetic algorithm to propose a decomposition of user stories into microservices.

The remainder of this paper is organized as follows, Sect. 2 related works; Sect. 3 Methodology and evaluation methods used; Sect. 4 our approach; Sect. 5 discussing results; and Sect. 6: Summarizes our conclusions.

2 Related Works

Methods and techniques have been proposed to define the granularity of microservices, for example:

Service Cutter a method and tool framework for service decomposition [7]. In Service Cutter approach, coupling information is extracted from software engineering artifacts. Its approach is more for SOA applications. Hassan and Bahsoon [8] propose microservice ambients, which use "aspects" to define the adaptation behavior needed to support changes in granularity at runtime. Hasselbring and Steinacker [9], to achieve adequate granularity, propose a vertical decomposition in self-contained systems throughout the business services. Gouigoux and Tamzalit [10] explain that choice of granularity should be based on the balance between the costs of quality assurance and the cost of deployment. Baresi et al. [11] propose Microservices Identification Through Interface Analysis (MITIA), they address the problem of granularity by proposing an automated process to identify candidate microservices through a light semantic analysis, independent of the domain of the concepts in the input specification concerning a reference vocabulary. They perform an analysis of the semantic similarity of the functionalities described in OpenApi. Tyszberowicz et al. [12] describe a systematic approach to identify microservices in the initial design phase that is based on specification the functional requirements of the system and that uses functional decomposition. Abdullah et al. [13] design a method to automatically decompose a monolithic application into microservices to improve the scalability and performance. They use the application's access logs and an unsupervised machine learning method, scale weighted k-means. De Alwis et al. [14] mathematically define a business system and a microservices-based system, then define heuristics to identify microservices. They propose a microservice discovery algorithm. Mazlami et al. [15] present a Graph-based clustering algorithm and a Class-based extraction model for the extraction of microservices from monolithic software architecture based on source code. Chen et al. [16] propose a top-down decomposition approach driven by data flows of business logic. Taibi and Syst [17] propose a process-mining approach to identify business processes in an existing monolithic solution based on three steps. In the first step, a process-mining tool is used to identify business processes. In the second step, processes with common execution paths are clustered and a set of microservices. In the third step, they propose a set of metrics to evaluate the decomposition quality. Jin et al. [18] propose Functionality-oriented Service Candidate Identification (FoSCI) framework to identify service candidates from a monolithic system, through extracting and processing execution traces. Microservices API patterns (MAP) [19] define some design and implementation patterns.

The above methods are mainly used in migrations from monoliths to microservices. The use of artificial intelligence is a subject of great interest, being the clustering algorithms the most used. Few methods support development from scratch (greenfield development). Different input data have been used, such as use cases, OpenApi specification, source code, dataflow diagram, database, execution call graphs, execution logs, and execution traces; mainly these methods are used at design and development time. The proposed method is used at design time, it uses user stories as input data and focuses on agile software development, none of the identified methods focus on these aspects. We characterized the process of applications based on microservices in [20] and we used that development process in [21].

3   Methodology

Based on one approach proposed by Hevner et al. [22]. The artifact to be created is the intelligent model of specifying the granularity of microservices that are part of an application. DSR implies a continuous and iterative assessment of the proposed artifact. Figure 1 shows the research model.

1. Identify the problem. To identify the problem and its relevance, a review of the state of the art was developed, research gaps were identified and the research questions for this work were formulated.

2. Identify and adapt the metrics. A systematic literature review was done to identify metrics that can be used to define the granularity. Section 3 shows these metrics.

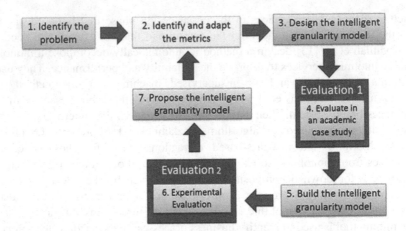

Fig. 1. Research model

3. Design the intelligent granularity model. A proposal of a formal specification of the granularity model can be found in Sect. 4.1. While a definition of a genetic algorithm for microservices decomposition is explained in Sect. 4.2

4. Evaluate in an academic case study. A state-of-the-art example called Cargo Tracking [11] was used to verify properly functioning and objectives compliance from our model. A comparison between results from the case of study and decomposition performed with DDD are shown in Fig. 4.

5. Build the intelligent granularity model. A genetic algorithm was implemented to generate the decomposition of the product backlog into microservices. An algorithm was implemented to evaluate metrics for decomposition. Sections 4 and 5 detail this implementation.

6. Experimental evaluation. Metrics of Cargo Tracking case study are analyzed by four methods: Domain-driven design (DDD), Service Cutter, Microservices Identification Through Interface Analysis (MITIA) [11] and our approach Microservices Backlog. Since DDD is the most widely used method for microservices identification, our first evaluation verified that obtained decomposition was consistent and close to that performed by DDD. A second evaluation compares decomposition made by our method versus other decompositions methods.

7. Propose the intelligent granularity model. Proposing intelligent granularity model. Based on metrics and analytical evaluation including adjustment through researching a Microservice Backlog is proposed as an intelligent specification and granularity evaluation model.

4   Our Approach

Agile practices are techniques used to control one aspect of the development process. One of the most widely used agile practices is Sprint/iteration planning [23], traditionally expressed in user stories within the product backlog. A model to define microservices granularity from user stories and analyze some metrics is proposed. A view of the model can be seen in Fig. 2.

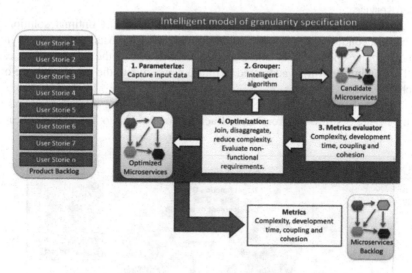

Fig. 2. Intelligent model of granularity specification

1. Parameterize. It is responsible for taking input data and converting it into a format that can be processed by the grouper. It extracts the key data, such as identifier, name, description, estimated points, estimated time, scenario, observations, and dependencies, from the user story. Later, with this data, the model can group the user stories in microservices and calculate the metrics. The format of the user stories is a JSON file or CVS where the key data are supplied.

2. Grouper. This component uses a genetic algorithm, which groups user histories into microservices, considering cohesion and coupling metrics, as well as the number of user stories associated with the microservice.

3. Metrics evaluator. This work considers the following metrics in the microservices backlog [3]: **1) Complexity – Points:** Estimated points of the effort needed to develop the user story. The story points are an indicator of the speed of development of the team. **2) Coupling – Absolute Importance of the Service (AIS):** The number of clients that invoke at least one operation of a microservice's interface [24]. **3) Coupling – Absolute Dependence of the Service (ADS):** The number of other microservices that microservice depends on. The number of microservices from which invokes at least one operation [24]. **4) Coupling – Microservices Interdependence (SIY):** Number of interdependent microservices pairs [24]. **5) Cohesion - Lack of cohesion (LC):** Measured as the number of pairs of microservices not having any dependency between them, adapted from [25]. LC of MS_i was defined by us as the number of pairs of microservices not having any interdependency between MS_i. **6) Weighted Service Interface Count (WSIC):** It is the number of exposed interface operations of the microservice [26]. For our model, a user story is related to an operation (one-to-one); so, we adapt this metric as the number of user stories associated wiht the microservice. **7) Development Time:** Estimated time of development in hours for the microservice. Summation of the estimated time of each user story that is part of the microservice.

4. Optimization. This optimizer allows finding the most optimal solution that meets certain conditions (non-functional requirements, test costs, cost of deployment, etc.), performing operations of union and decomposition of the microservices candidates. This optimizer will be addressed in future work, due to the time and scope of the research.

5. Outputs of the model. The calculated metrics and the microservices backlog diagram. Figure 3 shows Microservices Backlog for the Cargo Tracking application.

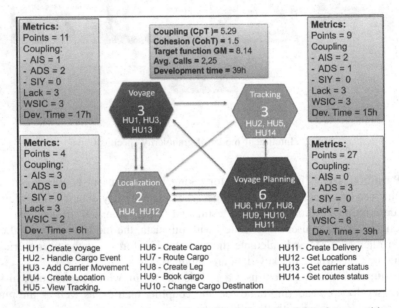

Fig. 3. Microservices backlog for Cargo Tracking using DDD decomposition

The microservices backlog in Fig. 3 was obtained by decomposition using DDD and the next steps: 1) The user stories were loaded. 2) The dependencies between the stories were defined. 3) The entities were identified. 4) The aggregates were defined, 5) The delimited contexts were established, the entities and their respective user histories were associated. 6) The metrics were calculated by the evaluator. Specific metrics for each microservice and the whole application. It can be highlighted that the grouper component of our model automatically identifies the candidate microservices, then the steps 3 to 5 are automatic.

From the model, the designer can see the size of each microservice, as well as its complexity, dependencies, coupling, cohesion, and development time. The architect can notice at first sight that the orange microservice is a critical point of the system if this microservice failure, then the whole system can fail because it is used by all the others. The architect at design time can already think about fault tolerance mechanisms, load balancing and monitoring on that critical microservice. They can have a vision of the global system in design time.

4.1 Formal Specification of the Granularity Model

Specification formal of the granularity model will be given in terms of the metrics stated in the previous section and by the target function (GM). It is intended to MINIMIZE (GM). GM is defined below. Let microservice-based application MSBA as:

$$MSBA = (MS, MT) \tag{1}$$

Where MS is a set of microservices, $MS = \{MS_1, MS_2, \ldots MS_n\}$ and MT is a set of the metrics calculated for MSBA. Then:

$$MS_i = (HU, MTS) \tag{2}$$

Where MS_i is the ith microservice, HU is the set of user stories associated with the ith microservice, then $HU = \{HU_1, HU_2, \ldots, HU_m\}$. MTS is a set of metrics calculated for MS_i. In this case, the calculated and used metrics in the model correspond to the coupling (CpT), the cohesion (CohT) and the number of stories associated with the microservice (WsicT). These metrics are defined below.

Coupling Metrics. Coupling is defined by three metrics: 1) absolute importance of the service (AIS), 2) absolute dependence of the service (ADS), and 3) microservices interdependence (SIY). These metrics are calculated based on the dependencies of the user stories for each microservice.

AIS_i is the number of clients invoking at least one operation of MS_i. At the system level, the AIS vector is defined, which contains the calculated AIS value for each microservice. To calculate the total value of AIS at the system level (AisT), the AIS vector norm is calculated. Thus:

$$\mathbf{AIS} = [AIS_1, AIS_2, \ldots, AIS_n] \tag{3}$$

$$AisT = |\mathbf{AIS}| \tag{4}$$

ADS_i is the number of other microservices on which the MS_i depends. To calculate the total value of ADS at the system level (AdsT), the ADS vector norm is calculated. Then:

$$\mathbf{ADS} = [ADS_1, ADS_2, \ldots, ADS_n] \tag{5}$$

$$AdsT = |\mathbf{ADS}| \tag{6}$$

SIY defines the number of pairs of microservices that depend bi-directionally on each other divided by the total number of microservices. At the system level, the vector SIY was defined:

$$\mathbf{SIY} = [SIY_1, SIY_2, \ldots, SIY_n] \tag{7}$$

$$SiyT = |\mathbf{SIY}| \tag{8}$$

Let the Cp vector as the system level coupling metric, calculating the norm of the vector Cp we have the coupling value for the application (CpT):

$$\mathbf{Cp} = [AisT, AdsT, SiyT] \tag{9}$$

$$CpT = |\mathbf{Cp}| \tag{10}$$

Cohesion Metric. In the same way, the cohesion for the ith microservice is defined by the metric lack of cohesion (LC), The degree of cohesion of each microservice is defined as the proportion of the Lack of cohesion metric divided by the total number of microservices that are part of the application.

$$Coh_i = LC_i/n \tag{11}$$

Where n is the number of microservices. At the system level, the vector **Coh** was defined, calculating the norm of the vector **Coh** we have the cohesion value for the application (CohT):

$$\mathbf{Coh} = [Coh_1, Coh_2, \ldots, Coh_n] \tag{12}$$

$$CohT = |\mathbf{Coh}| \tag{13}$$

Indeed, the MT vector is defined as follows:

$$\mathbf{MT} = [CpT, CohT, WsicT] \tag{14}$$

Where, CpT use (10), CohT use (13) and WsicT is defined as the highest WSIC value. We adapt WSIC as the number of user stories assigned to each microservice. Finally, the value of the target function GM use (14), it is defined as the MT vector norm.

$$GM = |\mathbf{MT}| \tag{15}$$

This mathematical expression allows us to determine how good or bad is the decomposition. The aim is to obtain a solution with low complexity, low coupling, and high cohesion. The genetic algorithm seeks to find the best combination, the best assignation of stories to microservices in such a way that GM is lower. The genetic algorithm is then designed as follows.

4.2   Genetic Algorithm for Microservices Decomposition

The genetic algorithms were established by Holland [27], it is iterative, in each iteration, the best individuals are selected, everyone has a chromosome, which is crossed with another individual to generate the new population (reproduction), some mutations are generates to find the optimal solution to the problem [28]. Our genetic algorithm consists in distributing or assigning user stories to microservices automatically, considering coupling and cohesion metrics. The implemented methods are explained below:

Get Initial Population Method. There is a set of user stories $HU = \{HU_1, HU_2, HU_3, ..., HU_m\}$, which must be assigned to the microservices. We have a set of microservices $MS = \{MS_1, MS_2, MS_3, ..., MS_n\}$ and some metrics calculated from the information contained in the user story. Individuals are defined from the assignment of stories to microservices, therefore, the chromosome of each individual is defined from an assignment matrix of ones and zeros, wherein the columns there are user stories and in the rows are the microservices, and the cross contains a 1 when the user story is assigned to the microservice or zero if not. In Table 1, an example is presented for 2 microservices $MS = \{MS_1, MS_2\}$ and 5 user stories $HU = \{HU_1, HU_2, HU_3, HU_4, HU_5\}$.

Table 1. Example of an assignment matrix

Microservices	HU1	HU2	HU3	HU4	HU5
MS_1	1	0	0	1	1
MS_2	0	1	1	0	0

The resulting chromosome would be the union of the assignments of each user story to each microservice, for this case, it would be: Chromosome: 10011 01100. From this chromosome, it is possible to define the function of adaptation or objective function, it uses (15).

Reproduction Method. A different assignment would be generated from selected parents. In our method, the father and mother are randomly selected from the population; to generate the child information is taken from the father and mother, from the assignment matrix the first columns of the father are taken, and the last columns of the mother are joined, generating a new assignment. It must be considered that a user story cannot be assigned twice, this means that in the assignment matrix only one can appear in each column. Example: Given the two chromosomes: 1) Father: 10011 01100. 2) Mother 01000 10111. The son would be 10000 01111.

Mutation Method. The mutation indicates changing a random bit of the chromosome, changing a bit of the chromosome of this problem from 1 to 0 or from 0 to 1, implies that a user story is assigned or unassigned to a microservice and this must be assigned or unassigned to another microservice. This implies that the mutation is done on two bits. Example: Mutate bit 7 of the obtained chromosome: 01011 10100. Mutated chromosome: 00011 11100. The mutated chromosomes must be included in the population. This process is carried out randomly, the individuals to be mutated are selected from the population, the mutation of a bit is also carried out randomly, for the mutation the value of the target function is calculated and included in the population.

Select Better Method: In the processes of genetic selection, the strongest survive, in the case of the problem of the automatic generation of the assignment of user histories to microservices, the n individuals who best adapt to the conditions of the problem survive. The assignments that imply a lower GM. The selection is made from the objective function, this is applied to each individual and the population is ordered in ascending form, considering the first places, the best individuals, corresponding to the assignments involving lower GM using (15).

Convergence: To determine the convergence of the method, the number of iterations or generations of the population to be processed is defined. At the end of the iterations, the algorithm is stopped, and the chromosome located in the first place is selected, which would be the best assignment of user stories to microservices. For the case studies used to evaluate the proposed method, a population of 1000 individuals were generated, with 100 iterations or generations, with 500 children and 500 mutations in each generation. The algorithm was tested several times obtaining the same result, even with more individuals and more iterations.

5   Results

The genetic algorithm was implemented in Java, to evaluate its results we use a case study and a quasi-experiment.

5.1   Evaluation in an Academic Case Study – Cargo Tracking Application

Baresi et al. [11] the describe Cargo Tracking application as follow, the focus of the application is to move a Cargo (identified by a TrackingId) between two Locations through a RouteSpecification. Once a Cargo becomes available, it is associated with one of the Itineraries (lists of CarrierMovements), selected from existing Voyages. HandlingEvents then trace the progress of the Cargo on the Itinerary. The Delivery of a Cargo informs about its state, estimated arrival time, and is on track. From the domain model proposed, we extracted and raised user stories and the product backlog is detailed in Table 2. The points and times are input data to the model. I this case they were estimated according to our experience and correspond to the effort and time involved in developing each user story.

A critical point of the proposed method is the dependencies between user stories. They must be identified and provided as input to the method, this information is included within the user stories. The parameterizing component offers functionality to define dependencies between user stories. We define a dependence between HU_i and HU_j when HU_i calls or executes HU_j. For example, to create a voyage (HU_1) you must get the locations (HU_{12}), this implies that the HU_1 has a dependence on HU_{12}. Table 3 presents the dependencies identified by us among the user stories. The dependencies were calculated according to the logic of the application understood by us. To illustrate the proposed genetic algorithm the statement of these dependencies is valid.

Table 2. Product backlog for Cargo Tracking application

ID	Name	Points	Estimated dev. time (hours)
HU_1	Create voyage	3	5
HU_2	Handle cargo event	3	5
HU_3	Add carrier movement	5	7
HU_4	Create location	2	3
HU_5	View tracking	3	5
HU_6	Create cargo	7	10
HU_7	Route cargo	5	7
HU_8	Create leg	2	3
HU_9	Book cargo	5	7
HU_{10}	Change cargo destination	1	2
HU_{11}	Create delivery	7	10
HU_{12}	Get locations	2	3
HU_{13}	Get carrier status	3	5
HU_{14}	Get routes status	3	5
Total		51	77

Table 3. User stories dependences

User stories	Dependences	User stories	Dependences
HU_1	$\{HU_{12}, HU_3\}$	HU_8	$\{HU_{12}\}$
HU_2	$\{HU_{12}\}$	HU_9	$\{HU_{12}\}$
HU_3	$\{HU_{12}\}$	HU_{10}	$\{HU_{12}\}$
HU_4	$\{\}$	HU_{11}	$\{HU_6, HU_{13}, HU_{14}\}$
HU_5	$\{\}$	HU_{12}	$\{\}$
HU_6	$\{HU_7, HU_9, HU_{11}\}$	HU_{13}	$\{HU_5\}$
HU_7	$\{HU_8\}$	HU_{14}	$\{HU_5\}$

Dependencies are used to calculate the metrics, for example, to calculate the AIS metric of the decomposition obtained with DDD for the microservice called Localization (see Fig. 4). MS_1 (Voyage) $= \{HU_1, HU_3, HU_{13}\}$, MS_2 (Tracking) $= \{HU_2, HU_5, HU_{14}\}$, MS_3 (Localization) $= \{HU_4, HU_{12}\}$, MS_4 (Voyage Planning) $= \{HU_6, HU_7, HU_8, HU_9, HU_{10}, HU_{11}\}$. AIS is the number of clients that invoke at least one operation of a microservice's interface. Then we count the number of microservices that invoke or use HU_4 o HU_{12} from the dependencies. HU_4 is not used by any other user stories, it does not appear in any dependencies (See Table 3), while HU_{12} is used by HU_1, HU_2, HU_3. HU_8, HU_9, and HU_{10} corresponding to 3 microservices, therefore AIS = 3. Similarly, other metrics are calculated.

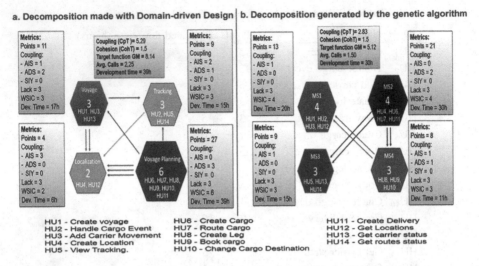

Fig. 4. Microservices backlog for the result of the DDD vs genetic algorithm.

Figure 4 presents the microservice backlog for the decompositions generated by the genetic algorithm compared with DDD for Cargo Tracking. Our method obtained the same number of microservices, this being an important approximation to DDD. Our method does not consider the semantic similarity between user stories. For example, HU_4 and HU_{12}, both are related to the Localization concept, as they are concepts related to the same, they must be associated with the same entity and therefore to the same microservice. In our method those stories were assigned in separate microservices, so they do not have any dependence between them (i.e. HU_4 has not dependence with HU_{12}). The decomposition performed by our method is different from DDD, our model does not group the entities and their stories or operation that make up the aggregate into a microservice.

With the decomposition obtained with the genetic algorithm, the critical point of failure of the proposed DDD solution is removed, Localization microservice is used for all microservices. The number of calls between microservices is reduced, thus improving performance. The maximum number of operations associated with a microservice is also reduced, as well as the estimated development time. In the decomposition generated by genetic programming, two microservices can function independently without depending on other microservices. Whereas in the solution proposed by DDD, one microservice can function independently. In the decomposition proposed by DDD, there are more dependencies. Therefore, the proposed model and the genetic algorithm considerably improves the decomposition and identification of microservices. To generalize this result, validation must be carried out in future work with more complex case studies specifically with real industry cases.

By distributing user stories differently, shorter development times of the entire system can be obtained. Considering that each microservice is developed by an independent team in parallel.

5.2 Quasi-Experimental Evaluation

To evaluate the results obtained by the model of specification of the granularity, we use the work done by Baresi et al. [11], they propose a decomposition to microservices of the Cargo Tracking case study using interface analysis and semantic similarity (MITIA), they also propose the decomposition of that same case using Service Cutter, we take those results and propose an experiment to compare our model with these methods, we include the decomposition performed by DDD. Also, we include a hypothetical case where only one user story was added per microservice, we call it 14MS, this corresponds to the case of the finest granularity, additionally, we include the monolithic solution. MITIA and Service Cutter propose the result of the decomposition in a domain model from there we determine the association of user stories and microservices. We use a quasi-experiment for evaluating our method against the other methods. The definition of the quasi-experiment is detailed below.

Scope: Compare the granularity specification model with the decomposition methods selected from the state of the art (DDD, Service Cutter, MITIA, 14MS and monolithic) for the Cargo Tracking case study. The GM granularity metric is evaluated in the decompositions obtained with each method to determine the accuracy of the proposed model. GM is calculated from coupling metrics, cohesion and number of operations assigned to each microservice.

Planning. 1) Objects of study: Microservices Backlog, DDD, Service Cutter, MITIA, 14 MS, and monolithic solution. 2) Independent variables: User stories dependences, decomposition obtained by each method. 3) Dependent variables: GM, Metrics: AisT, AdsT, SiyT, CpT, CohT, and number of microservices.

Hypothesis Formulation. H_0: Our microservices backlog model does not present a better decomposition in microservices, therefore the value of GM is greater than GM of the other methods, then the application has not better coupling and cohesion. **H_1:** Our microservices backlog model presents a better decomposition in microservices, therefore the value of GM is lower than GM of the other methods, then the application has better coupling and cohesion.

Operation. The quasi-experiment is carried out in the laboratory, the decomposition for the Cargo Tracking case study is determined for each one of the methods (see Table 4). Based on the dependencies of the user histories, the metrics are calculated and the value of GM for each decomposition (see Table 5). Another set of metrics were calculated for better analysis (see Table 6).

Analysis & Interpretation. The data collected correspond to the values calculated for the metrics and the GM function for each one of the methods compared. From the results obtained for each metric, the lowest and highest value is identified, to evaluate the hypotheses proposed. The data and hypothesis raised are simple and their validation does not require additional statistical analysis. Rejecting the H_0 hypothesis indicates that the decomposition proposed by our model is better than the decomposition proposed by the other methods.

Experiment Results and Discussions. First, the decomposition obtained by each of the methods is detailed. Table 4 shows these results. Second, we tabulate the results obtained for each metric. these can be seen in Table 5. Finally, we identify the methods that obtained lower and higher values for each metric including GM.

MITIA considers the semantic similarity between the operations, for that reason a distribution closer to DDD can be appreciated. The Service Cutter has one less microservice, but the distribution is like DDD, although the number of operations exposed by MS_3 is greater. Based on the calculated metrics, it can be appreciated that our decomposition presents a smaller coupling compared to the other methods. In this case, the cohesion is given in terms of the number of microservices that are part of the application, having more microservices this value will be greater; for this reason, the highest cohesion is presented by the decomposition with 14MS. But the value of the cohesion of our method is equal to that obtained with DDD and greater than Service Cutter and MITIA.

Table 4. Comparison of the decompositions of the methods evaluated

ID	Number of microservices	Microservices decomposition
Our approach: microservices backlog	4	$MS_1 = \{HU_1, HU_2, HU_3, HU_{12}\}$ $MS_2 = \{HU_4, HU_6, HU_7, HU_{11}\}$ $MS_3 = \{HU_5, HU_{13}, HU_{14}\}$ $MS_4 = \{HU_8, HU_9, HU_{10}\}$
DDD	4	$MS_1 = \{HU_1, HU_3, HU_{13}\}$ $MS_2 = \{HU_2, HU_5, HU_{14}\}$ $MS_3 = \{HU_4, HU_{12}\}$ $MS_4 = \{HU_6, HU_7, HU_8, HU_9, HU_{10}, HU_{11}\}$
Service cutter	3	$MS_1 = \{HU_4, HU12\}$ $MS_2 = \{HU_2, HU5\}$ $MS_3 = \{HU_1, HU_3, HU_6, HU_7, HU_8, HU_9,$ $HU_{10}, HU_{11}, HU_{13}, HU_{14}\}$
MITIA	4	$MS_1 = \{HU_3, HU_9, HU_{10}, HU_{13}\}$ $MS_2 = \{HU_1, HU_2, HU_5, HU_{11}, HU_{14}\}$ $MS_3 = \{HU_6\}$ $MS_4 = \{HU_4, HU_7, HU_8, HU_{12}\}$

As future work, other cohesion metrics will be considered and revised to be more precise in their calculation. Our method presents the lowest number of user stories or operations associated with a microservice (WsicT), with a value of 4 stories. The highest value is presented by Service Cutter with 10 stories associated with a single microservice, thus Service Cutter has a greater complexity of both implementation and operation.

Table 5. Metrics calculated for the decompositions of the methods evaluated

Metrics	Methods					
	14MS	DDD	Service cutter	MITIA	Our approach	Monolith
Number of MS	14	4	**3**	4	4	1
AisT	6.93	3.74	2.24	4.24	1,73	0
AdsT	5.48	3,74	2.24	4.69	2,24	0
SiyT	1.41	0	0	2,45	0	0
Coupling CpT	8.94	5.29	3.16	6.78	**2.83**	0
Cohesion CohT	3.44	**1.5**	1.15	1.06	**1.5**	0
WsicT	1	6	10	5	**4**	14
GM	9.63	8.14	10.55	8.49	**5.12**	14

Table 5 shows that the value of the GM obtained by our model is lower than all the other methods analyzed, additionally, the coupling (CpT) was the lowest, with the fewest number of stories associated with a microservice (WsicT), the cohesion (CohT) was the highest compared to DDD, Service Cutter, and MITIA. Therefore, we reject the H_0 hypothesis, which indicates that the decomposition proposed by our model is better than the decomposition proposed by the other methods, in terms of the metrics proposed in this work. The value obtained in the GM function for the monolithic application is the highest, in the same way, the GM value for 14MS is not the lowest, the appropriate solution is an intermediate point between the finest granularity (14MS) and the thickest granularity (Monolith), therefore, the mathematical formalization fits the expected.

Also, we calculate other metrics to evaluate the proposed methods: **1) Points:** Greater number of story points associated with a microservice. **2) Average of Calls:** that indicates the average of calls that a microservice makes to another microservice. **3) Development time:** Each user story has an associated estimated development time, therefore the estimated development time of the MS_i is the sum of the development time of each user story associated with the MS_i. Table 6 shows these metrics.

Table 6. Other metrics for microservices backlog

Metrics	14MS	DDD	Service cutter	MITIA	Our approach	Monolith
Max. points	7	27	41	19	21	52
Avg. calls	1.14	2.25	2.67	3	1.50	0
Dev. time (hours)	10	39	61	30	30	77

The lowest number of story points without considering the metrics calculated for 14 MS corresponds to MITIA with 19 points. The shortest development time was the decomposition proposed by MITIA with 30 h. Our method obtains one close value of 21 points and 30 h of development respectively, being these values better than DDD and Service Cutter. The average number of calls of our approach is less than DDD, Service Cutter, and MITIA. This metric measure or determine the degree of dependence that have the microservices that are part of the application, a larger value implies a greater dependence and lower performance because they require the execution of operations that belong to other microservices in other containers.

6 Conclusions

This paper proposes the Microservices Backlog a genetic-programming technique that calculates at design time each microservices' granularity. This model uses as inputs the user stories expressed in the product backlog, to decompose the functionalities or requirements of the application into microservices. To evaluate our proposal, the case study Cargo Tracking was used, the decomposition made with DDD, service Cutter and Microservices Identification Through Interface Analysis (MITIA) were compared. The decomposition performed by our model has less coupling, greater cohesion, fewer operations associated with a microservice, a better average of calls from one microservice to another and lower value in the proposed objective mathematical function (GM) used in the genetic algorithm. This algorithm allows us to model and evaluates the level of granularity of the microservices that are part of the application at design time.

To model and define the right granularity we identify and adapt metrics of complexity: estimated story points; metrics of coupling: absolute importance of the service (AIS), absolute dependence of the service (ADS), microservices interdependence (SIY); metrics of cohesion: lack of cohesion (LC) and degree of cohesion (CohT); and metrics of size of the microservice: weighted service interface count (WSIC). These metrics were used to determine the most suitable decomposition with less coupling, high cohesion, and fewer assigned user stories. Mathematical formalization of an application based on microservices in terms of user stories and metrics was proposed. Too coarse-grained microservices could lead to significant drawbacks, while too fine-grained services could increase the system's overall complexity and performance, our model found the right service granularity at design time, based on the mathematical function proposed GM for the genetic program.

References

1. Villamizar, M., Garcés, O., Castro, H., Verano, M., Salamanca, L., Gil, S.: Evaluating the monolithic and the microservice architecture pattern to deploy web applications in the cloud. In: 10th Computing Colombian Conference, pp. 583–590 (2015)
2. Soldani, J., Tamburri, D.A., Van Den Heuvel, W.-J.: The pains and gains of microservices: a systematic grey literature review. J. Syst. Softw. **146**, 215–232 (2018)
3. Bogner, J., Wagner, S., Zimmermann, A.: Automatically measuring the maintainability of service- and microservice-based systems. In: Proceedings of the 27th International Workshop on Software Measurement and 12th International Conference on Software Process and Product Measurement on - IWSM Mensura 2017, pp. 107–115 (2017)
4. Zimmermann, O.: Microservices tenets: agile approach to service development and deployment. Comput. Sci. Res. Dev. **32**(3–4), 301–310 (2017)
5. Jamshidi, P., Pahl, C., Mendonca, N.C., Lewis, J., Tilkov, S.: Microservices: the journey so far and challenges ahead. IEEE Softw. **35**(3), 24–35 (2018)

6. Beck, K., Fowler, M.: Planning Extreme Programming. Addison Wesley, Boston (2001)
7. Gysel, M., Kölbener, L., Giersche, W., Zimmermann, O.: Service cutter: a systematic approach to service decomposition. In: Aiello, M., Johnsen, E.B., Dustdar, S., Georgievski, I. (eds.) ESOCC 2016. LNCS, vol. 9846, pp. 185–200. Springer, Cham (2016). https://doi.org/10.1007/978-3-319-44482-6_12
8. Hassan, S., Ali, N., Bahsoon, R.: Microservice ambients: an architectural meta-modelling approach for microservice granularity. In: Proceedings - 2017 IEEE International Conference on Software Architecture, ICSA 2017, pp. 1–10 (2017)
9. Hasselbring, W., Steinacker, G.: Microservice architectures for scalability, agility and reliability in e-commerce. In: Proceedings - 2017 IEEE International Conference on Software Architecture Workshops, ICSAW 2017: Side Track Proceedings, pp. 243–246 (2017)
10. Gouigoux, J.P., Tamzalit, D.: From monolith to microservices: lessons learned on an industrial migration to a web oriented architecture. In: Proceedings - 2017 IEEE International Conference on Software Architecture Workshops, ICSAW 2017: Side Track Proceedings, pp. 62–65 (2017)
11. Baresi, L., Garriga, M., De Renzis, A.: Microservices identification through interface analysis. In: De Paoli, F., Schulte, S., Broch Johnsen, E. (eds.) ESOCC 2017. LNCS, vol. 10465, pp. 19–33. Springer, Cham (2017). https://doi.org/10.1007/978-3-319-67262-5_2
12. Tyszberowicz, S., Heinrich, R., Liu, B., Liu, Z.: Identifying microservices using functional decomposition. In: Feng, X., Müller-Olm, M., Yang, Z. (eds.) SETTA 2018. LNCS, vol. 10998, pp. 50–65. Springer, Cham (2018). https://doi.org/10.1007/978-3-319-99933-3_4
13. Abdullah, M., Iqbal, W., Erradi, A.: Unsupervised learning approach for web application auto-decomposition into microservices. J. Syst. Softw. **151**, 243–257 (2019)
14. De Alwis, A.A.C., Barros, A., Polyvyanyy, A., Fidge, C.: Function-splitting heuristics for discovery of microservices in enterprise systems. In: Pahl, C., Vukovic, M., Yin, J., Yu, Q. (eds.) ICSOC 2018. LNCS, vol. 11236, pp. 37–53. Springer, Cham (2018). https://doi.org/10.1007/978-3-030-03596-9_3
15. Mazlami, G., Cito, J., Leitner, P.: Extraction of microservices from monolithic software architectures. In: 2017 IEEE International Conference on Web Services (ICWS), pp. 524–531 (2017)
16. Chen, R., Li, S., Li, Z.: From monolith to microservices: a dataflow-driven approach. In: 2017 24th Asia-Pacific Software Engineering Conference (APSEC), pp. 466–475 (2017)
17. Taibi, D., Systä, K.: From monolithic systems to microservices: a decomposition framework based on process mining. In: International Conference on Cloud Computing and Services Science - CLOSER 2019, no. March (2019)
18. Jin, W., Liu, T., Cai, Y., Kazman, R., Mo, R., Zheng, Q.: Service candidate identification from monolithic systems based on execution traces. IEEE Trans. Softw. Eng. (2019)
19. Zimmermann, O., Stocker, M., Zdun, U., Lübke, D., Pautasso, C.: Microservice API Patterns (2019). https://www.microservice-api-patterns.org/introduction. Accessed 17 Dec 2019
20. Vera-Rivera, F.H.: A development process of enterprise applications with microservices. J. Phys: Conf. Ser. **1126**(17), 012017 (2018)
21. Vera-Rivera, F.H., Vera-Rivera, J.L., Gaona-Cuevas, C.M.: Sinplafut: a microservices – based application for soccer training. J. Phys: Conf. Ser. **1388**(2), 012026 (2019)
22. Bichler, M.: Design science in information systems research. MIS Q. **28**(1), 75–105 (2006)
23. Versionone Enterprise, "13 Anual State of Agile Report" (2018). http://stateofagile.com/#ufh-i-521251909-13th-annual-state-of-agile-report/473508

24. Rud, D., Schmietendorf, A., Dumke, R.R.: Product metrics for service-oriented infrastructures. In: Conference: Applied Software Measurement. Proceedings of the International Workshop on Software Metrics and DASMA Software Metrik Kongress (IWSM/MetriKon 2006) (2006)
25. Candela, I., Bavota, G., Russo, B., Oliveto, R.: Using cohesion and coupling for software remodularization: is it enough? ACM Trans. Softw. Eng. Methodol. 25(3), 1–28 (2016)
26. Hirzalla, M., Cleland-Huang, J., Arsanjani, A.: A metrics suite for evaluating flexibility and complexity in service oriented architectures. In: Feuerlicht, G., Lamersdorf, W. (eds.) ICSOC 2008. LNCS, vol. 5472, pp. 41–52. Springer, Heidelberg (2009). https://doi.org/10.1007/978-3-642-01247-1_5
27. Holland, J.: Adaptation in Natural and Artificial Systems. University of Michigan Press, Michigan (1975)
28. Herrera, F., Lozano, M., Verdegay, J.L.: Algoritmos Genéticos: Fundamentos, Extensiones y Aplicaciones. ProQuest (1995)

Automated Web Service Specification Generation Through a Transformation-Based Learning

Mehdi Bahrami$^{(\boxtimes)}$ and Wei-Peng Chen

Fujitsu Laboratories of America, Sunnyvale, CA, USA
{mbahrami,wchen}@fujitsu.com

Abstract. Web Application Programming Interface (API) allows third-party and subscribed users to access data and functions of a software application through the network or the Internet. Web APIs expose data and functions to the public users, authorized users or enterprise users. Web API providers publish API documentations to help users to understand how to interact with web-based API services, and how to use the APIs in their integration systems. The exponential raise of the number of public web service APIs may cause a challenge for software engineers to choose an efficient API. The challenge may become more complicated when web APIs updated regularly by API providers. In this paper, we introduce a novel transformation-based approach which crawls the web to collect web API documentations (unstructured documents). It generates a web API Language model from API documentations, employs different machine learning algorithms to extract information and produces a structured web API specification that compliant to Open API Specification (OAS) format. The proposed approach improves information extraction patterns and learns the variety of structured and terminologies. In our experiment, we collect a sheer number of web API documentations. Our evaluation shows that the proposed approach find RESTful API documentations with 75% accuracy, constructs API endpoints with 84%, constructs endpoint attributes with 95%, and assigns endpoints to attributes with an accuracy 98%. The proposed approach were able to produces more than 2,311 OAS web API Specifications.

Keywords: Web API service · REST API · Natural language processing · Machine learning

1 Introduction

Web Application Programming Interface (API) [13] exposes data and software functions to third-parties or subscribed users. Web APIs can be reached locally or remotely by using REpresentational State Transfer (REST) [23] which is a software architecture style that divides platform and programming language. The web service REST APIs are core technology of software integration and it

© Springer Nature Switzerland AG 2020
Q. Wang et al. (Eds.): SCC 2020, LNCS 12409, pp. 103–119, 2020.
https://doi.org/10.1007/978-3-030-59592-0_7

has been used widely in cloud-based services and the Internet-of-Things (IoT) devices. In addition, a third-party is able to efficiently integrate an external functions or data through REST APIs in own native software applications.

API publishers charge users based on their number of API calls, usage of API, or a flat rate. For instance, an API publisher may provide a range of free API calls (e.g., 1000 free API calls per day) and charge additional fee for the additional requests.

The power of APIs enable a web service provider to offer information without sharing its own implementation. Different hardware devices also may use APIs to expose their functionality and their internal data. For example, web APIs in Internet-of-Tings (IoT) allows users to read or access data from a connected device [11].

1.1 Motivation

This study aims answer to the following questions. (i) How we can construct API specification from API documentation by employing machine-learning technology? (ii) Is the approach scalable to apply the process to a variety of APIs?

With the rise in number of web APIs in the market, manually understanding of all APIs and their endpoints is not only labor intensive but also it is an error prone task for software engineers. Web APIs might be revised or updated periodically, when it creating a significant overheads for software engineers to keep track of all changes.

In a digital business when major digital services rely on different third-party platforms, web API economy is the key point for determining the value of provided services. Software engineers need to choose the best web APIs for developing a reliable and cost effective service, which requires web API evaluation by reading the API documentations. This concern raises several questions, *How software engineers find all relevant web APIs? How software engineers automatically can evaluate web APIs without reading lengthy web API documentations?* The answer is accessing a machine-readable API specification. However, it raises another challenge when majority of API providers do not have any standard API specification.

In order to understand the variety of APIs in a standard format, we can employ machine-learning to construct API specification. API Specification can be used for automated API validation, automated API monitoring and automated API quality assessment [16]. An API Specification which aims to be generated by machine, allows software engineers to use automation on analyzing, validating and code synthesis to generate software application. Machine-generated API specification may also help API provider to offer better services such as automated API testing when machine read API documentations and validate information automatically. API specification opens door to a set of new technologies such as automated service integration when all required specifications have been defined by machine.

1.2   Related Works

Although there are some existing standardization initiatives around API specification to produce a machine readable API specification but only major API providers offers this type of format for their API specifications. API providers may offer Open API Specification (OAS), YAML which is a human-friendly and cross language machine readable format. Our goal in this study is to provide a platform that produces OAS from any API documentations. Therefore, our approach should be able to understand the variety of APIs.

There are also some studies around producing API specifications. For instance, Robillard et al. [20] presented a field study by performing survey and in-person interview to recommend how to design API documentations. However, this study does not provide an automated approach to produce API specification.

Although the title of a study by Gu et al. [10] is similar to our work, it is not an information extraction platform. The authors present a natural language query-based platform to find API usage.

Zhong et al. [25] defined a method to create specification for Java APIs which cannot be applied to REST API documentations. In another study, [7] shown a composition architecture for API description. In a recent study, [24] enriches API Guru by constructing API endpoints. However, our study focuses on a variety of API documentations without considering a predefined OAS. Another alternative option is using web annotation to construct API specification which is explained by Bahrami et al. [3]. Our approach in this paper employs several machine learning algorithms to mitigate software engineers' issues by mining a large number of API documentations. It extracts information and constructs OAS API Specifications for more than 2,311 APIs. Once we have a large number of API specification, the API OAS file can be used to produce other artifact such as automated API validation, automated code generation and API recommendation.

This paper organized as follows. In the next section, we describe i) API Corpus (Sect. 2.2) construction that includes a web-crawler and a REST API Filter (Sect. 2.3) which uses a logistic-regression for filtering out non-REST API documentations; ii) Information Extraction (Sect. 2.6) that uses an API Language Model (Word2Vec) and transformation-based learning algorithm; Table Extraction (Sect. 2.8) extracts HTML table tags and it constructs a SVM model to detect API attributes (e.g., parameter); Sect. 3 defines our datasets and evaluation results of each component. Finally, Sect. 4 summarizes this study.

2   Proposed Approach

Our proposed approach consist of an end-to-end platform with different components. Figure 1 shows the key component of the proposed approach. Our goal is extracting information from API documentations which is published by API providers.

2.1 Parallel Web Crawler

In the first step, we collect a massive number of API documentations. By collecting a large number of API documentations, first, it allows us our proposed machine learning algorithm to learn from a variety of data that enables the platform to learn different API documentations with different structures. Second, the proposed method learns from a volume of data that improves the accuracy of information extraction. We use a parallel web crawler to collect a massive number of API documentations which have been published by API providers. It stores HTML file on a local disk.

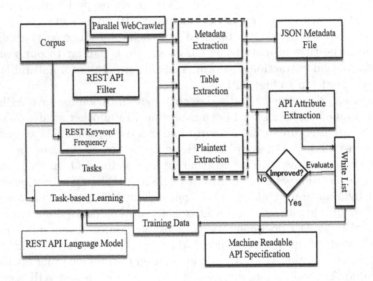

Fig. 1. An overview of the key component of the proposed approach

2.2 API Corpus

API corpus is a collection of HTML pages of API documentations which are collected by parallel web-crawler agents.

2.3 REST API Filter

This component allows API Learning to filter out the non-REST pages from API Corpus. The REST API Filter employs a logistic regression model which explained by [22] to detect REST API documentations. For each API documentations we generate an array of k REST keywords where key_j^k represents the term frequency of jth keyword in each document doc_i. The following equation shows the logistic regression function. It is a linear classification model which classifies the REST content and non-REST contents of collected HTML pages.

$$F(x) = \frac{1}{1 + e^{-(tf(doc_i, key_j^k) - th)}} \tag{1}$$

In Eq. 1, tf represents the linear function of variable doc (term frequency) for each API documentations and key_j^k that indicates each key_j in kth REST keywords. It clusters pages into REST or non-REST API documentations.

2.4 Tasks

In order to extract information from *API Corpus*, we have a set of rule-based regular expression patterns for different tasks. Each task includes an initial regular expression pattern for the given task. For example, a task may define a regular expression to extract *API endpoint* or to extract *default value, maximum and minimum values* of a parameter. Each initial regular expression pattern can be improved iteratively through a transformation-based learning [18]. In a related study, [12] define a model to train a regular expression pattern to improve the acceptance of a language per positive sample cases, authors apply some restriction rules to the initial regular expression but it cannot extend the initial regular expression. In our proposed method, we use both extension phase (by using *API Language Model* and other rules) to extend the initial pattern, and reduction phase that uses restriction rules to improve the pattern for accepting of a language for a given task.

2.5 API Language Model

API Language Model is defined as a neural language model [5] that shows probability distribution on all sentences in *API Corpus*. It uses embedding of words to predict word sequences and it is defined as follows.

$$\sum_{-k \leq j-1,\, j \leq k} \log P(w_{t+j}|w_t) \tag{2}$$

k denotes the previous words, j denotes the current word. Since this is a domain-specific information extraction task, we cannot use existing language models because it adds noise for our information extraction which is explained in Sect. 2.6. To retrieve a similar word from the language model, we use a cosine similarity [8] which measures the similarity of two words, $W_{1,i}$ and $W_{2,i}$ based on their vector representations where $i = [1..n]$ in defined API language model of n APIs. By computing the similarity from the language model, it allows us to retrieve all synonyms terminologies of (e.g., $W_{1,i}$) which have been used in *API Corpus* by different APIs.

2.6 Learning Diverse Extraction

We define several information extraction **tasks** where each task corresponds to extraction a single information from API documentation. Accumulation of output of all tasks (**trained model**) provide API specifications. In addition, we use some tasks of trained model to categorize information. For example, a task may classify the content of a table as a *response type* or a *parameter type*.

We defined a set of positive and negative examples for each task. Each task has an initial regular expression pattern and it is defined manually but it is improved iteratively when it learns different positive and negative examples. We use transformation-based learning where it consists of two phases that include **extension phase** and **reduction phase**. In order to train a model that applies different regular expression patterns to each task, we need to update the initial regular expression pattern and expend the constant words which have been used in initial pattern. The main target of two phases processing is updateing the pattern. The second target is updating constant words which have been used in initial patter because different API providers may require different patterns to extract the same information in OAS (e.g., API endpoints). A trained task should be trained based on both positive and negative examples. For instance, Facebook uses the terminology of *fields* to describe the input parameters of an endpoint[1]; but Google uses *parameters* to describe the input parameters of an endpoint[2].

By using *API Language Model* we can find synonymous of given constant words from initial pattern (e.g., parameter) and add *fields* as an equivalent terms in task definition. In this example, the final trained regular expression task should be able to extract *fields* from Facebook API documentations and *parameters* from Google API documentations. It can construct API specification for both APIs. In the OAS of each API specification, the trained task can extract both relevant information and constructs OAS parameters as: $paths \rightarrow endpoint \rightarrow HTTP\_Verb \rightarrow parameters$.

We develop a novel approach based on transformation-based learning as explained in Fig. 2 that i) expends the acceptance of initial regular expression (RE) pattern, and then, it reduces the RE pattern to only matched positive sample cases to minimize the acceptance of negative sample cases. After completion of both phase, the final RE pattern learned from both positive and negative examples; therefore, the task can provide a common RE pattern that maximizes the positive cases and minimizes the negative cases. In addition, since different API providers use a variety of terminologies for a single word, a constant regular expression is not capable to learn efficiently all synonyms words. We use *API Language Model* that finds all synonyms words according to API Corpus, then it applies the new set of synonyms words for each constant of RE pattern. The model learns new words in addition to original constant that improves acceptance of positive examples and reduces negative examples.   Each OAS API Specification consist of several objects, such as API metadata (e.g., title, description), endpoints, attributes, responses, and etc. Therefore, we need a set of different tasks to extract information and produce a structured based OAS file (JSON). The following tasks shows some examples of *IE Tasks* in API Learning.

i) API Endpoint extraction task provides the key information of a REST API and it provides a URL for an API endpoint along with its HTTP verb;

---

[1] See https://developers.facebook.com/docs.
[2] See https://developers.google.com/+/web/api/rest.

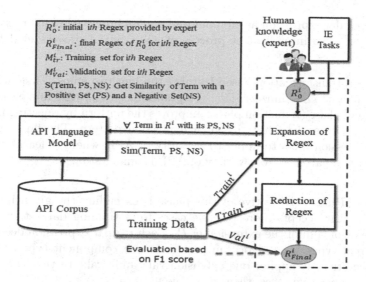

Fig. 2. Learning diverse extraction framework

ii) Parameter attribute extraction returns a list of input/output parameter and security information of an API endpoint. It also includes some specific sub-tasks such as a minimum value of a parameter, a maximum value of a parameter, the default value of a parameter and etc. Therefore, the method need to understand and classify the content of HTML tables to recognize input parameters, output parameter and etc. For each task we need a method to detect and extract information from API documentation. We use regular expression to define different task extract. The problem statement of information extraction from API documentations can be defined for a target API ($\mathcal{A}$). Our goal is to extract a set of positive sample case and avoid negative sample cases that can be extracted from an API documentations. Let $s_{p,i}$ be the set of i positive sample case and $s_{n,j}$ be the set of j negative sample case. It can be defined as $s_{p,i} \in L$ where $i \in \{1, ..., m\}$; and $s_{p,i}$ denotes a set of m positive sample case of language $L_{\mathcal{A}}$ for the target APIs($\mathcal{A}$); and $s_{n,j} \notin L_{\mathcal{A}}$ where $j \in \{1, .., n\}$; and $s_{n,j}$ denotes n negative sample cases of language $L_{\mathcal{A}}$. ($L_{\mathcal{A}}$ represents acceptance language of target APIs, $\mathcal{A}$). f_P defines a function that uses a set of regular expression patterns P, that accepts $s_{p,i}$ sample cases and rejects $s_{n,j}$ in $L_{\mathcal{A}}$. Our objective function can be defined as $\max_{x \in \mathbb{C}} f_P(x)$ where C denotes the API documentations that can be retrieved from *API Corpus*. We can summarize the objective function as follows.

$$\max_{x \in \mathbb{C}} f_P(|s_p(x_{\mathcal{A}})| - |s_n(x_{\mathcal{A}})|) \tag{3}$$

In this equation, we maximize acceptance of the positive sample cases f_P where it removes the negative sample cases of $s_n(x_{\mathcal{A}})$ for different APIs ($\mathcal{A}$); and $\mathcal{A} \in \{1, .., n\}$ where n denotes the total number of APIs. It takes an initial regular expression as an input and find an improved regular expression as output. The improvement process of given initial process id defined in Sect. 2.6.

We use a transformation-based learning through two steps. First, we define extension phase to maximize f_{P_i} the acceptance more positive sample cases, and in the second phase (reduction phase) improves the pattern by rejecting negative sample cases for a given initial regular expression pattern. The final improved regular expression aims to apply to majority of APIs where it learns different structured and patterns from variety of API documentations.

Extension Phase. Objective of this phase is extending the given initial RE pattern P_0 that accepts more positive cases from training dataset, τ. Table 1 shows the algorithm of the extension of P_0. Each regular expression decomposes into different types. The algorithm processes each component type as follows. In each iteration, it applies one extension rule and evaluate the pattern, if it accepts more positive cases, then revise the pattern.

i) *charTerm*: This type of RE component refers to string values (e.g., *default*) and can be extended by similarity extension or character extension method as follows.

    a) Similarity extension. It uses the similarity of *charTerm* component (Line 2 in Table 1) by inquiring the value of *charTerm* to *API Language Model*. The model uses *cosinesimilarity* function to return similar terms based on the vector representation of *charTerm* in *API Corpus*; and then, it adds each return value with an *OR* operation with a pair of parenthesis to $P_i(charTerm)$.

    b) Character extension. It applies all possible uppercase and lowercase of a *charTerm* in each iteration (Line 3 in Table 1). API specification is case sensitive, we cannot replace all words as lowercase or as uppercase characters. For example, '*POST*' in REST API documentations shows that this term is referring to a *HTTP verb function* and it is completely different to '*post*' or '*Post*' which are regularly used in English language.

ii) *Range*: This type of RE component refers to a set of range values (e.g., *[1–4]* accepts number between 1 to 4).

iii) *RE Component Replacement*: This type of RE component decomposes each RE component into one or multiple RE components. Each component of a RE pattern can be replaced with its equivalent RE if acceptance of positive sample cases is equal or better than $P_i - 1$. For example, $[a-zA-Z]$ can be replaced with $([a-z]|[A-Z])$.

Reduction Phase. The objective of reduction phase is removing unnecessary accepted pattern elements from *newPattern* (returned pattern from *ExtensionPhase*). As shown in Table 1, the algorithm takes a set of positive and negative sample cases, s_p and s_n, respectively. It returns a new pattern, P_i

Table 1. Extension and reduction algorithms

---

pattern_extension()

Input: a set of positive sample cases s_p,
a set of negative sample cases s_n,
previous regular expression pattern, P_{i-1}.
Output: extended pattern, $newPattern$.

1: for each $CharTerm$ in P_{i-1}:
2:   $P_i(charTerm) = Smilar(charTerm, \alpha)$
3:   $P_i(charTerm) = CharExtension(charTerm)$
4: for each $openParenthesis$ in P_{i-1}:
5:   $P_i(openParenthesis) =$
    $starExtension(openParenthesis)$
6: for each range in P_{i-1}:
7:   $P_i(range) = increaseRange(range)$
8: for each component in P_{i-1}:
9:   $P_i(component) =$
    $regexTransformation(component)$
10: if $f_{P_i}(x) > f_{P_{i-1}}(x)$:
11:   $newPattern = f_{P_i}$
12: else:
13:   $newPattern = f_{P_{i-1}}$
14: return $newPattern$

---

pattern_reduction()

Input: a set of positive sample cases s_p,
a set of negative sample cases s_n,
extension pattern, $P_\tau = pattern\_extension(P_{i-1})$.
Output: a new pattern, P_i

1: $P_i = P_\tau$
2: for each $ORcomponent$ in P_τ:
3:   $P_{tmp} = dropOR(element)$
4:     if $val(P_\tau) \geq val(P_{tmp})$:
5:       $P_i = P_{tmp}$
6: for each $range$ in P_τ:
7:     $P_{tmp} = rangeRestriction(range)$
8:     if $val(P_i) \geq val(P_{tmp})$:
9:       $P_i = P_{tmp}$
10: for each $charTerm$ in P_τ:
11:     $P_{tmp} = charTermRestriction(charTerm)$
12:     if $val(P_\tau) \geq val(P_{tmp})$:
13:       $P_i = P_{tmp}$
14: return P_i

that can be used in substitute of *newPattern* (P_τ). *i) OR reduction*: In this phase we remove each component if it does not decrease the acceptance rate of positive cases.

ii) range restriction: Some ranges can be removed or shrank when it does not change the validation rate.

iii) character restriction: It restricts the acceptance of characters. For instance, *"POST \b+ (URI\URL)"* can be restricted to *"POST \b[1,1000](URI\URL)"*, if the validation rate did not decrease by revising the pattern; then it can be decreased to a lower number in each iteration (i.e., *"POST \b[1,999](URI\URL)"*). By performing both phases through several iterations, the final pattern learns majority of sample cases. It satisfies the following conditions: i) maximizes acceptance rate of positive sample cases; ii) minimizes the rejection of positive sample cases: iii) maximizes the acceptance rate of rejection of negative sample cases; and iv) minimizes the acceptance rate of negative sample cases.

2.7 Metadata Extraction

Metadata of an API is one of the set of extraction tasks. For instance, the API title, API security protocol, and API host address. This component generates a set of extracted information and add them into the structured data (*info, host* in OAS file).

2.8 Table Extraction

Most of the API documentations uses HTML table tags to explain list of endpoints, attributes (e.g., parameters). Each HTML table tag may consist of different OAS objects, such as parameters, responses, security, and security definition.

2.9 Plain Text Extraction

Some API providers describe their information as a flat HTML page which means does not have some sort of semi-structured data, such as HTML table tags. The API publisher may use both HTML table tags and plain-text flat description to transfer their information to the readers. This component extracts information from plain text information.

2.10 API Attribute Extraction

Component generates a set of different endpoint's attributes, such as minimum value of a parameter, maximum value of a parameter, default value of a parameter and etc. **White List** contains both manual annotation and automated API validations which is created by calling the API and it contains the results of API endpoint response. The final output is a **Machine Readable OAS API Specification** for each API.

3   Experiment

We implemented all described components of API Learning.

3.1   API Corpus Construction

We used several sources to collect a comprehensive list (pointer list) of APIs, such as ProgrammableWeb, API Harmony, Rapid API, API Guru and etc. We use API title and API documentations URL from the list. Each source may also consist of other metadata information of an API. The pointer list consists of more than 20,000 APIs and some of the information might be incorrect (e.g., incorrect API Doc URL or a generic API title). In this experiment, we have to process the content to fix incorrect information and we target REST APIs. We used *Scrapy*[3] for implementation of the parallel web-crawler. We consider a web-crawler that composes of 32 parallel web-crawler agents. Table 2 shows the size of *API Corpus* in different experiments. We show only some example of different experiments for data acquisition with different maximum deep level of URL extractions and maximum of page per APIs.

Table 2. API corpus size of different experiments

Exp#	*MaxDepth*	*MaxPage*	# of files	Size-GB
17	5	1,000	2,822,997	208.6
20	4	100	148,479	8.3
35	3	300	156,497	7.4
37	4	300	256,583	15.0

Table 3. An example of query of top 7 most similar words to a positive word of ['POST']

HTTP	Prediction	HTTP	Prediction
GET	**0.867**	Request	0.668
DELETE	**0.828**	Endpoint	0.639
PUT	**0.777**	URI	0.639
PATCH	**0.746**		

Table 4. Detection of REST API documentations

Class	Precision	Recall	F1
Positive REST page	0.91	0.93	0.92
Negative REST page	0.89	0.86	0.88
Average	0.91	0.91	**0.91**

---

[3] https://scrapy.org/.

3.2   API Language Model

We use Word2Vec which is described by Mikolov et al. in [15] and [14]. We cleaned the API Corpus by removing scripts and HTML tags to produce the model. API Language model allows the method to understand semantic definition of each word. We use Gensim [19] to create a Word2Vec [9, 21] from *API Corpus*. By providing a set of positive and/or negative words, we may inquiry the model to find similar words. For example, Table 3 shows the synonyms words of *'POST'* in *API Corpus* for top 7 words. This result clearly shows that our API Language Model can successfully detect synonyms words from API documentations where it is trained based on API Corpus. The parameter of Word2Vec is described by Rong in [21]. We chose 300 for the window size which represents the maximum windows distance between a selected word and a predicted word within a sentence. The rest of the parameters of *API Language Model* shown in Table 5.

3.3   Information Extraction

In order to extract information, we defined several tasks with initial pattern of RE as described in Sect. 2.6. Some defined patterns have been used for table extraction and detecting table mapping as described in Sect. 2.8. Figure 3 shows a comparison between acceptance of $R_0 \in L_A$ and $R_{final} \in L_A$ for 5 different tasks. The average of iteration in these tasks to achieve (R_{final}) is 14. Table 4 shows 5 different tasks as follows. *Default Value*: learns template to extract default values of a parameter; *Maximum Value*: learns a template to extract maximum value of a parameter; *Optional Parameters*: learns a template to find whether is optional or mandatory; *Parameter Description*: learns a template to extract parameter description section (e.g., heading title of the section); *Introduction block of output parameter*: learns a template to detect if a section corresponds to output parameters of an API (e.g., heading title of a section). Table 4 shows the given input (P_0) to algorithms and shows the result after processing extension and reduction phase as output (P_{final}) which corresponds

Table 5. Hyper parameters of API language model

# of sentences: 10,140,000

# of words: 23,103,011

# of word types: 1,580,559

# of unique words (after word types drops): 213,167

# of windows in CBOW: 300

Min. count=5 (training parameter)

Min. count leaves 20,960,959 word corpus (90% of original)

downsampling leaves estimated 18,603,396 word corpus

# of parallel workers: 64

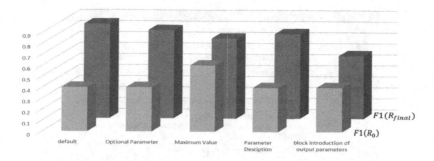

Fig. 3. A comparison between F1 evaluation of R_0 (baseline) and R_{final}

to improved regular expression through the transformation-based learning. As shown in Fig. 4, both the word token (new terminologies) and new pattern have been updated according to *API Language Model*, *RE* extension phase and *RE* reduction phase. By performing on more positive and negative sample cases, (P_{final}) can be improved. After applying (P_{final}) of each task to the *API Corpus*, the proposed platform generates a set of extracted information as a JSON file for each API which includes: i) API metadata, ii) API endpoints, and iii) HTML tables that corresponds to API attributes. The defined tasks helps us to extract different OAS objects but our ultimate goal is using extracted information to interact with APIs. We use two strategies to evaluate our extracted information. First, we annotated the extracted information for a large number of APIs, that includes API endpoint and tables. Second, we perform API call to validate the extracted information which can be applied to all extracted endpoints. In the first approach of evaluation, We annotated 200 APIs that consist of 1,780 extracted tables (API endpoint attributes), and extracted endpoints for 350 APIs that consist of 2,929 endpoints. To the best of our knowledge this large number of annotation of API documentations have been collected for the first time. Each annotation shows that whether an API endpoint extracted correctly from the source or not. The same annotation completed for HTML table to check whether the produced structured file (JSON format) of HTML table is correct or is not correct. We correctly extracted 86.75% of API endpoints and 81.29% of table according to annotated information $(Avg = \mathbf{84.02\%})$. Second, our automated API validation applies to all extracted API endpoints that contain 54,873 endpoints and check the response code. It shows that 76% of endpoints were valid.

We use Scikit-Learn to train a logistic-regression [1] model with L1 penalty to detect REST API documentations. We create an annotation tools based on Selenium [2] that allows a user to quickly annotate API documentations by using a semi-automated platform. The Selenium browser automatically open different API documentations from pointer list and a user manually annotates API documentations as: i) relevant to REST API documentations (*Positive Class*); ii) relevant but explaining different API documentations (*Reference Class*); or, iii) irrelevant to REST API (*Negative Class*). We train the model with considering

Task	State	RE
Default Value	P_0	(default{1,2}value)(.*)(\d|\w+)
	P_{Final}	(.*(default|usually|always|type){1,2}.*(value|attribute|parameter|namespace))(.*)((\d|-)+)
Maximum value	P_0	((maximum value(.*)\d)|(range(.*)\d(.*)\d))
	P_{Final}	(((max|decimal) (value|result)(.*)\d)|((certain)(.*)\d((\W \w)*)\d))
Optional Parameter	P_0	(is required|is necessary|required|necessary|is mandatory|is not optional)"
	P_{Final}	((processing) (names)|(processing) (defined)|(names)|(defined)|(processing) (loaded)|(processing) (bill) (record))"
Param. Desc.	P_0	(parameters|names|titles|subjects|params)
	P_{Final}	((models)|(dates)|(descriptions|ingredients)|(regular)|(testmod))
Introduction block of out. param/	P_0	(output (parameter|parameters))
	P_{Final}	((output|result|returned|calculated|signature) (mode|feature|gene)|(tags|form|items|param|proper|models)))

Fig. 4. Sample tasks of learning about API specifications

three classes as well as only positive/negative classes (reference pages considered as part of positive class). Due to page limitation, Table 4 shows only the performance of the model for detecting positive pages versus negative pages.

Table 6. OAS-based table type detection training dataset

Type	#	Type	#
Parameters	5,979	Response	6,290
Security	8,225	Security definition	150

We also collect a set of available OAS-based API specifications as ground-truth from different API providers who offers OAS JSON files, such as Spotify and API directories, such as API Guru. We train a SVM model with the following configuration by using Scikit-learn [17] package in Python. *penalty=l2, dual=False, tol=1e−3* The model trains with 14,450 data points (70% of dataset) as shown in Table 6. The model predicts four different table types from testing dataset (6,194 data points; 30% of dataset) with an accuracy of **95%**. The next step is assigning tables according to their predicted type (e.g., parameter) to API endpoints, which defines API endpoint attributes. We use a page segmentation algorithm that assigns extracted endpoints to their attributes according their appearance in API documentations (e.g., a table attribute appears after endpoint). We evaluate this assignment process manually for correctness of assignment of 223 API endpoints to their attributes. In this annotated dataset, only 3 out of 223 of assignment were incorrect that defines an accuracy of **98.65%** of the assignments of attributes to API endpoints. API Learning at the end produces 2,311 API specifications and consolidate information with other available OAS resources which produces 3,311 API specifications and it showcases in our API directory. A partial sample OAS file that collected from our proposed approach is shown in Fig. 5. In addition we deployed the valid APIs in Fujitsu RunMyProcess platform[4]. A demonstration of the previous study and deployment can be found in Bahrami et al. [4] and Choudhary et al. [6]. The deployed APIs can be accessible through Fujitsu RunMyProcess platform where users are able to efficiently design and test a web-based software application by accessing a large number of public APIs.


```
{
 - info: {
      Category: "Social",
    + Tags: [...],
      API Architecture: "REST",
      Description: "The Twitter Search Tweets API provides low-latency, full-fidelity, query-based access to the previous 30 days of Tweets wi
    - privacy: {
         Terms Of Service URL: "https://twitter.com/en/tos"
      },
    + x-versions: {...},
      Support: "https://support.twitter.com/",
      versions: { },
      API Validation: "OAuth 2, Shared Secret, Token",
      Secondary Category: "Search, Tweets",
      API Type: "Web/Internet",
    - social: {
         Twitter URL: "https://twitter.com/TwitterDev"
      },
      Device: "No",
      title: "Twitter Search Tweets API",
      Homepage: "https://developer.twitter.com/en/docs/tweets/search/api-reference"
   },
 - paths: {
    - statuses/mentions_timeline: {
       + get: {...}
      },
    - geo/search: {
       - get: {
          - parameters: [
             - {
                  Operator: "keyword",
                - Description: {
                     Text: "Matches a keyword within the body of a Tweet. This is a tokenized match, meaning that your keyword string wil
                   - Attribute: {
                        example: " a tweet with the text "i like coca-cola" would be split into the following tokens: i, like, coca, col
                     }
                  }
               }
            ]
         }
      },
```


Fig. 5. A partial snapshot of a produced API specification in OAS format that collected from different sources and API documentation

Table 7 shows a comparison between our approach and D2Spec as a related work [24]. The results of our approach shows that our approach is scalable when it construct 73% correct API endpoints from a sheer number of API endpoints (54,873). Our approach also capable to extract parameter, detect the type of parameters where the related work is only limited to API endpoint construction. Although the performance of endpoint extraction is equal to our results, the total number of extracted endpoints and APIs are much smaller than our outcomes (22% of our 54,873 endpoints). We also evaluate the API endpoints with using API call and API match to our ground through (existing) OAS files.

---

[4] Available at: https://www.runmyprocess.com.

Table 7. Comparison of related works

Feature	D2Spec (Yang et al. 2018)	Our approach
# of labeled APIs	120	200
Endpoint evaluation method	Endpoint matching	Manual annotation, API call
# of generated API Spec.	120	**1,923**
# of Endpoints	2,486	**54,873**
Endpoint evaluation	84% (22% of our dataset)	84%
Parameter extraction	No	**Yes**
Parameter type detection	No	**81.29%** Acc.

4   Conclusion

In this paper, we introduced a novel framework that collects a large number of API documentations. Our web crawler collected more than 20,000 APIs and we targeted REST APIs. We used a logistic regression model to detect REST API documentations. The framework processes all collected HTML pages as an *API corpus* and generates an *API Language Model* to understand the variety of terminologies of different API documentations. The proposed approach improves a set of information extraction regular expression patterns by extending the acceptance of sample cases and reducing elements that do not improve the acceptance rate. We used the improved patterns to extract OAS objects. We extracted HTML table tags and each table type detected by a SVM model and produces OAS API attributes. Our experimental results show that we have successfully extracted API specification from heterogeneous API documentations with an accuracy of 84%.

References

1. Abney, S.: Semisupervised Learning for Computational Linguistics. Chapman and Hall/CRC, Boca Raton (2007)
2. Automation, S.B.: Selenium ide (2014)
3. Bahrami, M., Chen, W.P.: WATAPI: composing web API specification from API documentations through an intelligent and interactive annotation tool. In: 2019 IEEE International Conference on Big Data (Big Data), pp. 4573–4578. IEEE (2019)
4. Bahrami, M., Park, J., Liu, L., Chen, W.P.: API learning: applying machine learning to manage the rise of API economy. In: Companion Proceedings of the The Web Conference 2018, pp. 151–154 (2018)
5. Bengio, Y., Ducharme, R., Vincent, P., Jauvin, C.: A neural probabilistic language model. J. Mach. Learn. Res. **3**(Feb), 1137–1155 (2003)
6. Choudhary, S., Thomas, I., Bahrami, M., Sumioka, M.: Accelerating the digital transformation of business and society through composite business ecosystems. In: Barolli, L., Takizawa, M., Xhafa, F., Enokido, T. (eds.) AINA 2019. AISC, vol. 926, pp. 419–430. Springer, Cham (2020). https://doi.org/10.1007/978-3-030-15032-7_36

7. Cremaschi, M., De Paoli, F.: Toward automatic semantic API descriptions to support services composition. In: De Paoli, F., Schulte, S., Broch Johnsen, E. (eds.) ESOCC 2017. LNCS, vol. 10465, pp. 159–167. Springer, Cham (2017). https://doi.org/10.1007/978-3-319-67262-5_12

8. Dehak, N., Dehak, R., Glass, J.R., Reynolds, D.A., Kenny, P.: Cosine similarity scoring without score normalization techniques. In: Odyssey, p. 15 (2010)

9. Goldberg, Y., Levy, O.: Word2vec explained: deriving Mikolov et al'.s negative-sampling word-embedding method. arXiv preprint arXiv:1402.3722 (2014)

10. Gu, X., Zhang, H., Zhang, D., Kim, S.: Deep API learning. In: Proceedings of the 2016 24th ACM SIGSOFT International Symposium on Foundations of Software Engineering, pp. 631–642. ACM (2016)

11. Hou, L., Zhao, S., Li, X., Chatzimisios, P., Zheng, K.: Design and implementation of application programming interface for internet of things cloud. Int. J. Netw. Manag. 27(3), e1936 (2017)

12. Li, Y., Krishnamurthy, R., Raghavan, S., Vaithyanathan, S., Jagadish, H.: Regular expression learning for information extraction. In: Proceedings of the Conference on Empirical Methods in Natural Language Processing, pp. 21–30. Association for Computational Linguistics (2008)

13. Masse, M.: REST API Design Rulebook: Designing Consistent RESTful Web Service Interfaces. O'Reilly Media, Inc., Sebastopol (2011)

14. Mikolov, T., Chen, K., Corrado, G., Dean, J.: Efficient estimation of word representations in vector space. arXiv preprint arXiv:1301.3781 (2013)

15. Mikolov, T., Sutskever, I., Chen, K., Corrado, G.S., Dean, J.: Distributed representations of words and phrases and their compositionality. In: Advances in Neural Information Processing Systems, pp. 3111–3119 (2013)

16. Myers, B.A., Stylos, J.: Improving API usability. Commun. ACM 59(6), 62–69 (2016)

17. Pedregosa, F., et al.: Scikit-learn: machine learning in python. J. Mach. Learn. Res. 12(Oct), 2825–2830 (2011)

18. Ramshaw, L.A., Marcus, M.P.: Text chunking using transformation-based learning. In: Armstrong, S., Church, K., Isabelle, P., Manzi, S., Tzoukermann, E., Yarowsky, D. (eds.) Natural Language Processing Using Very Large Corpora. TLTB, vol. 11, pp. 157–176. Springer, Dordrecht (1999). https://doi.org/10.1007/978-94-017-2390-9_10

19. Rehurek, R., Sojka, P.: Gensim-python framework for vector space modelling. NLP Centre, Faculty of Informatics, Masaryk University, Brno, Czech Republic, vol. 3, no. 2 (2011)

20. Robillard, M.P., Deline, R.: A field study of API learning obstacles. Empir. Softw. Eng. 16(6), 703–732 (2011)

21. Rong, X.: Word2vec parameter learning explained. arXiv preprint arXiv:1411.2738 (2014)

22. Schmidt, M., Le Roux, N., Bach, F.: Minimizing finite sums with the stochastic average gradient. Math. Program. 162(1–2), 83–112 (2017)

23. Thomas, R., et al.: Architectural styles and the design of network-based software architectures. University of California, Irvine (2000)

24. Yang, J., Wittern, E., Ying, A.T., Dolby, J., Tan, L.: Automatically extracting web API specifications from HTML documentation. arXiv preprint arXiv:1801.08928 (2018)

25. Zhong, H., Zhang, L., Xie, T., Mei, H.: Inferring resource specifications from natural language API documentation. In: Proceedings of the 2009 IEEE/ACM International Conference on Automated Software Engineering, pp. 307–318 (2009)

Performance Evaluation on Blockchain Systems: A Case Study on Ethereum, Fabric, Sawtooth and Fisco-Bcos

Rui Wang[1,2], Kejiang Ye[1(✉)], Tianhui Meng[1], and Cheng-Zhong Xu[3]

[1] Shenzhen Institutes of Advanced Technology, Chinese Academy of Sciences,
Shenzhen 518055, China
{rui.wang2,kj.ye,th.meng}@siat.ac.cn
[2] University of Chinese Academy of Sciences, Beijing 100049, China
[3] State Key Laboratory of IoT for Smart City, University of Macau, Zhuhai,
Macao, Special Administrative Region of China
czxu@um.edu.mo

Abstract. Blockchain technology is currently receiving increasing attention with widely used in many fields such as finance, retail, Internet of Things, and intelligent manufacturing. Although many blockchain applications are still in the early stage, this technique is very promising and has great potential. Blockchain is considered as one of the core technologies to trigger a new round of disruptive changes after Internet. In the future, it is expected to change the development prospects of many industries. However, the current blockchain systems suffer from poor performance which affects large-scale application. In order to better understand the performance of the blockchain systems, in this paper, we analyze four mainstream blockchain systems (Ethereum, Fabric, Sawtooth and Fisco-Bcos), and then perform a performance comparison through open source blockchain benchmarking tools. After that, we propose several optimization methods and discuss the future development of blockchain technique.

Keywords: Blockchain · Ethereum · Fabric · Sawtooth · Fisco-Bcos

1 Introduction

Blockchain is essentially a distributed ledger technique. It is the core technology of Bitcoin [1] and other virtual currencies. It can record transactions between buyers and sellers and ensure that these records are verifiable and permanently stored. At present, according to different application scenarios and user needs, blockchain can be divided into three categories: public blockchain, private blockchain, and consortium blockchain.

The *public blockchain* is the most decentralized blockchain. These public blockchains, such as Bitcoin and Ethereum [2], are not controlled by third-party organizations. Everyone can access the data records on the chain, participate in transactions, and compete for the right to generate new blocks. Program developers have no right to interfere with the users, and each participant (i.e. node) can join and exit the network freely, and perform particular operations.

Q. Wang et al. (Eds.): SCC 2020, LNCS 12409, pp. 120–134, 2020.
https://doi.org/10.1007/978-3-030-59592-0_8

The *private blockchain* is completely the opposite. The write permission of the network is fully controlled by an organization or institution, and the data access is regulated by the organization. It can be understood as a weakly centralized system. Because the participating nodes is few and have strict restrictions. Compared with public blockchains, the time for private blockchains to reach consensus is relatively short, the transaction speed is faster, the efficiency is higher, and the cost is lower. This type of blockchain is more suitable for internal use by specific institutions, such as the Linux Foundation [3].

The *consortium blockchain* is a blockchain between the public and private blockchains, which can achieve "partial decentralization". Each node on the chain usually has a corresponding physical institution or organization; participants authorize to join the network and form a stakeholder alliance to jointly maintain the blockchain operation. Similar to private blockchain, consortium blockchain has the characteristics of low cost and high efficiency and is suitable for B2B transactions such as transactions and settlement between different entities.

Due to the different design, these blockchains have different application scenarios. Table 1 compares the three different blockchain systems. The public blockchain is suitable for scenario that has high requirements on credibility and security, which does not require high transaction speed. Private blockchain or consortium blockchain is more suitable for applications with high requirements on privacy protection, transaction speed and internal supervision. The consortium blockchain's transaction confirmation time and transactions per second are greatly different from the public blockchain, and the requirements for security and performance are also higher than the public blockchain.

Table 1. Comparison of public, private and consortium blockchain

	Public blockchain	Private blockchain	Consortium blockchain
Participants	Free	Permissioned	Permissioned
Features	Completely decentralized Poor performance High fault tolerance	Trusted centralization High performance Low fault tolerance	Partially decentralized Moderate performance Moderate fault tolerance
Use cases	Cryptocurrency	Audit, Issuance	Payment, Settlement
Project	Bitcoin, Ethereum	ConsenSys	Hyperledger fabric

For example, *Ethereum* is one of the most well-known public blockchains. It provides a decentralized Ethereum Virtual Machine to process peer-to-peer contracts through its dedicated cryptocurrency Ether. *Hyperledger* [4] is the representative of the consortium blockchain. As an open consortium, Hyperledger has incubated a series of business blockchain technologies, including a distributed ledger framework, a smart contract engine, a client library, a graphical interface, a utility library, and a sample application. The current blockchain system cannot solve the impossible triangle problem of "Decentralization, Scalability and Security" [27], so we need to find a balance point to take the advantages of different blockchain systems.

In order to better understand the performance of different blockchain systems, in this paper, we analyze four mainstream blockchain systems (Ethereum, Fabric, Sawtooth and Fisco-Bcos), and then perform a performance comparison through open source blockchain benchmarking tools.

The contributions are summarized as follows:

1. A detailed performance comparison of Ethereum, Fabric [5], Sawtooth [6] and Fisco-Bcos [7] is presented.
2. Major performance bottlenecks are revealed.
3. Some future optimization methods are proposed.

The rest of the paper is organized as follows: Sect. 2 introduces the architectures of different blockchains. Section 3 describes the motivation and goals of our research. Section 4 introduces the experimental method. Section 5 presents the experimental results and proposed some possible optimizations; Sect. 6 introduces the related work. Finally, we conclude the whole paper and present the future work in Sect. 7.

2 Background: Blockchain Architecture

2.1 Ethereum

The blockchain is derived from bitcoin. Generally, we call it *blockchain 1.0*, which is mainly based on various electronic currencies. The most common industry applications are micropayments, foreign exchange, and so on. With the development of blockchain, *blockchain 2.0* has emerged. The usage scenarios of Blockchain 2.0 are also richer than Blockchain 1.0. It can not only be used in payments, but can also be used in stocks, bonds, futures, loans, mortgages, property rights, smart property and smart contracts. Bitcoin is the representative of blockchain 1.0, Ethereum is the representative of blockchain 2.0. Ethereum is a platform, including digital currency Ether and Ether-Script, which are used to build distributed applications. It can implement Turing-complete virtual machines and use any currency, protocol and blockchain. The overall architecture of Ethereum can be divided into three layers [26]: *underlying services*, *core layer*, and *top-level applications* (see Fig. 1).

The *underlying services* include P2P network services, LevelDB database, cryptographic algorithms, and basic services such as sharding optimization. Each node in a P2P network is equal and provides services together. Nodes in the network can generate or review new data. The Ethereum blocks, transactions, and other data are ultimately stored in the LevelDB database. Cryptographic algorithms are used to ensure the privacy of data and the security of the blockchain. Sharding optimization makes it possible to verify transactions in parallel.

The *core layer* contains core elements such as the blockchain, consensus algorithm, and Ethereum virtual machine. It takes blockchain technology as the main body, supplements Ethereum's unique consensus algorithm, and uses EVM (Ethereum Virtual Machine) to run smart contracts. This layer is the core component of Ethereum. The first problem that the decentralized ledger of the blockchain structure needs to solve is how to ensure the consistency and correctness of the ledger data on different

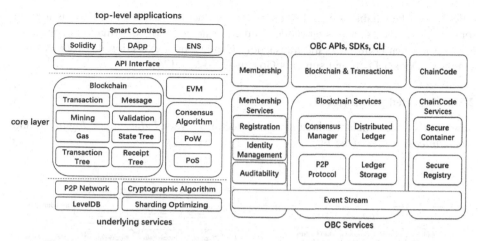

Fig. 1. Ethereum architecture.   **Fig. 2.** Fabric architecture.

nodes, and the consensus algorithm is used to solve this problem. EVM is a major innovation of Ethereum. It is the operating environment of smart contracts in Ethereum, which enables Ethereum to implement more complex logics.

The *top-level applications* include API interfaces, smart contracts, and Decentralized Application (DApp). Ethereum's DApp exchanges information with the smart contract layer through Web3.j. All smart contracts run on the EVM and use RPC calls.

Various layers cooperate with each other and perform their duties to form a complete Ethereum system. In the underlying services, data such as transactions and blocks are stored in the LevelDB database. Cryptographic algorithms are used to encrypt block generation and transaction transmission. Optimization of sharding speeds up transaction verification. The consensus algorithm is used to solve the consistency of the ledger among P2P network nodes. The DApp in the top-level application needs to be executed on the EVM.

2.2 Hyperledger Fabric

Figure 2 shows the architecture of Fabric. Member management [23] provides member registration, identity protection, content confidentiality, and transaction auditing functions. All members of OBC (Open Blockchain) must be licensed to initiate transactions, which is different from the public blockchain (all participants do not need to log in and can submit directly). When an OBC member initiates a transaction, if the Transaction Certificate Authority (TCA) function is enabled, the transaction certificate will protect the member ID from being seen by unrelated parties. Block services [28] are used to maintain a consistent distributed ledger throughout the network. Based on the P2P communication network (gRPC), messages are transmitted between nodes through HTTP messages. Highly optimized design makes the status synchronization efficient and reliable. Consensus algorithms (PoW [8], PoS [9], PBFT [10], Raft [11]) are modular and pluggable. OBC provides a CLI client tool to enable developers to quickly test the ChainCode [22] or query the transaction status. ChainCode is used to form a smart contract and is embedded in the transaction. All confirmation nodes must execute it when confirming the transaction. ChainCode's execution environment is a sandbox (Docker [12]) and supports Go, Java, Node.js [24].

2.3   Hyperledger Sawtooth

Sawtooth's design includes three main architectural layers: *ledger layer*, *log layer*, and *communication layer* (see Fig. 3):

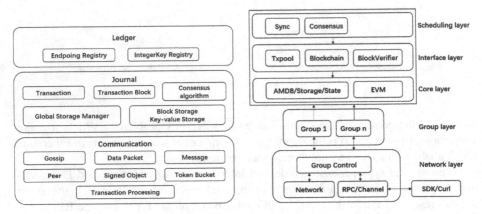

Fig. 3. Sawtooth architecture   **Fig. 4.** Fisco-Bcos architecture

The implementation of the *ledger layer* is basically completed by extending the functions of the log layer and the communication layer. For example, the two built-in Endpoint Registry and IntergerKey Registry transaction families, and the MarketPlace transaction family as an example, are derived by extending the underlying functions.

The *log layer* implements the core functions of Sawtooth. It implements consensus algorithms, transactions, blocks, global storage managers, and data storage (block storage and key-value storage). The block and transaction concepts are similar with other blockchain projects.

The *communication layer* mainly implements communication between nodes through the gossip protocol [13], which mainly includes protocol layer connection management and basic flow control. Nodes send messages to each other to exchange information. Information is usually encapsulated and transmitted in different types of messages, such as transaction messages, transaction block messages, and connection messages. Like many distributed systems, in the entire architecture, lots of messages need to be sent between nodes through a chat protocol. To this end, the communication layer implements a Token Bucket mechanism to control the transmission speed of data packets.

2.4   Fisco-Bcos

Fisco-Bcos' structure (see Fig. 4) is mainly divided into *network layer* and *group layer*. The network layer is mainly responsible for communication between blockchain nodes. The group layer is mainly responsible for processing intragroup transactions. Each group runs a separate ledger. In a network adopting a group architecture, there may be multiple different ledgers according to different business scenarios. Blockchain nodes can select groups to join according to business relationships and participate in the data sharing and consensus process of the corresponding ledgers.

The group architecture has good scalability. Once an organization participates in such a consortium blockchain, it has an opportunity to flexibly and quickly enrich business scenarios and expand business scale, and the system operation and maintenance complexity and management costs also linearly decrease. On the other hand, each group in the group structure independently executes the consensus process, and each group independently maintains its own transaction transactions and data without being affected by other groups. The advantage is that the groups can be decoupled, operate independently, and achieving better privacy isolation. When messages are exchanged across groups, authentication information is carried, which is credible and traceable.

3   Motivation

Nowadays, the poor performance is one of the main challenges of current blockchain technology. The performance indicators of the blockchain mainly include *transaction throughput* and *latency*. Transaction throughput represents the number of transactions that can be processed at a fixed time, and latency represents the response and processing time to transactions. In practical applications, two factors need to be comprehensively examined. It is incorrect to consider only transaction throughput without latency. Long-term transaction response will hinder user experience and affect users' experience. Considering latency without throughput will cause lots of transactions to be queued. Some platforms must be able to handle large amount of concurrent users. Technical solutions with low transaction throughput will be directly abandoned.

In order to solve the performance problems of the blockchain systems, we have conducted in-depth research on mainstream blockchain systems, mainly including the throughput, latency, and resource utilization of the blockchain systems. By analyzing the architecture and adjusting the corresponding parameters, we understand the characteristics of each blockchain system and find out the bottlenecks of the blockchain systems. After that, our goal is to adopt some optimization measures to alleviate these bottlenecks and improve the performance of blockchain systems.

4   Experimental Methodology

We use *transaction throughput* and *latency* as the main performance metrics to evaluate the performance of Ethereum, Fabric, Sawtooth, and Fisco-Bcos. Transaction throughput is the number of transactions that the system can process per second.

The specific calculation method is the number of concurrent transactions divided by the average response time. Latency is the time it takes for an application to send a transaction proposal to the transaction commit. We use *caliper* to load and test the blockchain system. Caliper [14] is a blockchain performance benchmarking framework that allows users to test different blockchain solutions using predefined use cases and obtain a set of performance test results. The Caliper project was originally launched in May 2017. Huawei, a global information and communication technology company, actively participated in the design and development of the project, which was accepted by the hyperledger technical committee and added to the hyperledger project.

All tests were run in the following environments: 4 identically configured servers with the Intel (R) Xeon (R) CPU E5-2630 v4 @ 2.20 GHz CPU, 64G DDR3 RAM, 4T HDD and running Ubuntu18.04 LTS. And our test consists of three phases:

- **Preparation stage:** In this stage, the main process uses the blockchain configuration file to create and initialize internal blockchain objects, deploy smart contracts according to the information specified in the configuration, and start monitoring objects to monitor the resource consumption of the back-end blockchain system.
- **Testing phase:** In this phase, the main process performs tests based on the configuration file. Caliper will generate tasks based on the defined workload and assign them to client child processes. Finally, the performance statistics returned by each client will be stored for subsequent analysis.
- **Reporting phase:** Analyze the statistics of all clients for each test round and generate reports.

During the testing phase, we tested these blockchain systems by selecting different system settings. Each test involves sending transactions from peers at a fixed rate, and these transactions are built in a docker container. Ethereum 1.2.1, Fabric 1.4.0, Sawtooth 1.0.5, Fisco-Bcos 2.0.0 have been tested.

5   Experimental Results

In this section, we have studied the impact of different system architectures on the performance of different blockchain systems. The TPS (Transactions Per Second) and latency obtained in the tests are the average values obtained after multiple tests.

5.1   Ethereum's Performance

We use the Ethereum adapter through caliper, which includes assembling connection profiles (also known as blockchain network profiles), using adapter interfaces from user callback modules; transaction data collected by the adapter, and completing examples of connection profiles. We prepare "*open*", "*query*" and "*transfer*" workloads for Ethereum. The "open" workload includes opening accounts and testing the writing performance of the ledger. The "query" workload includes querying accounts and testing the reading performance of the ledger. The "transfer" workload includes trading between accounts and testing the transaction performance of the ledger. All chaincodes to be tested must be installed on the channel and peer. Ethereum will separately set up accounts, query accounts, and conduct transactions at the same time.

First, we set the txNumber of "open", "query", and "transfer" to 100, 200, and 100, and then we continue to increase the Send Rate for testing. The results show that when we increase the Send Rate, the throughput of the query workload increases synchronously with the Send Rate. The open workload will reach a bottleneck when throughput reaches around 15, and it cannot continue to improve. The transfer workload will reach a bottleneck when the throughput reaches around 10 and cannot be further improved (see Fig. 5). In terms of latency, the query workload does not cause any latency. For the open workload and transfer workload, as the Send Rate increases, the latency will increase slightly, but it is not obvious (see Fig. 6). We also conduct corresponding tests by increasing txNumber, but the experimental results did not change significantly.

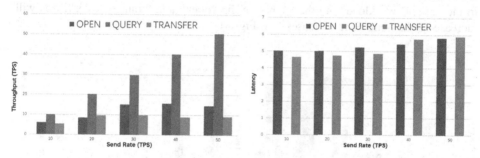

Fig. 5. Throughput of Ethereum with varying workload. **Fig. 6.** Latency of Ethereum with varying workload.

Discussion: Because the block production speed of Ethereum is fixed, one block is generated every 15 s, the TPS of Ethereum is determined by the number of transactions that can be packed in a block. Ethereum has no restrictions on blocks, but the speed of network broadcasts limits the size of blocks. If the block size is too large, the latency will become very high, resulting in network unavailability. At the same time, the total amount of gas in the block will also limit the number of packaged transactions. The total amount of gas used by all transactions in the block cannot exceed this limit. Therefore, before the Istanbul upgrade, the theoretical value of TPS for Ethereum is only 30. In view of the current situation, Ethereum needs to modify the architecture in order to greatly improve the TPS. Therefore, Ethereum 2.0 (aka Serenity) is being developed. Ethereum 2.0 contains many new features: sharding, proof of stake Casper, new virtual machine eWASM, and more. These new features are currently implemented in three phases: Phase 0 mainly implements the beacon chain. The main function of the beacon chain is to implement PoS and provide the basis for sharding. In Phase 1, Ethereum 2.0 will bring a shard chain. The shard chain is the key to the future scalability of Ethereum. It allows transactions to be executed in parallel. The beacon chain will also start managing multiple shards at this time. In phase 2, various functions are beginning to be integrated, the lighthouse chain and the shard chain have been activated, and state execution will be added in this phase.

5.2 Hyperledger Fabric's Performance

We deploy fabric1.4.0 to 3 physical machines. Each physical machine is regarded as an Organization. Each Organization has 2 peers. Endorsement policy: Any member of Org1MSP are acceptable. The database is GolevelDB [15]. We also use "open", "query" and "transfer" workloads for Hyperledger Fabric. Then we deploy caliper on the remaining machine. We set txNumber to 200, 400, 200 respectively, and at the same time, we continuously adjusted the batchsize and Send Rate for testing. The results show that when we fixed the batchsize to 20, by increasing the Send Rate, the TPS of the "query" workload increased linearly, the TPS of the "open" workload would reach the bottleneck around 100, and the TPS of the "transfer" workload would reach the bottleneck at around 50 (see Fig. 7). In terms of latency, there is almost no latency in the "query" workload, and the latency in the "open" and "transfer" workloads will increase as the Send Rate increases (see Fig. 8).

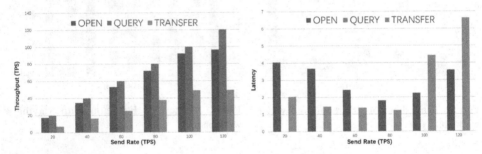

Fig. 7. Throughput of Fabric with varying workload (batchsize = 40).

Fig. 8. Latency of Fabric with varying workload (batchsize = 40).

Next, we adjust the batchsize to 40, 60, 80, 100, 120, and leave the rest of the settings unchanged. The results show that with the increase of Send Rate, "transfer" workload's TPS will increase with the increase of batchsize. When batchsize is larger than 100, TPS no longer grows linearly and reaches a new bottleneck (see Fig. 9). For the latency, under the condition that the batch size is unchanged, the latency of "transfer" will decreases with the increase of Send Rate before reaching the bottleneck of TPS, and the latency will increase with the increase of Send Rate after reaching the bottleneck of TPS. As the batch size becomes larger, the latency will gradually increase. When the TPS reaches the bottleneck, the latency is gradually reduced by the effect of the batchsize (see Fig. 10).

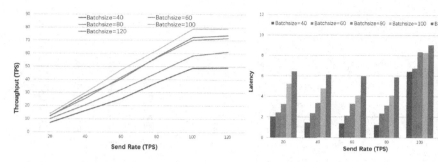

Fig. 9. Throughput of Fabric with different batchsize ("transfer" workload).

Fig. 10. Latency of Fabric with different batchsize ("transfer" workload).

Discussion: Through the experimental results, we can find that, in order to better improve the TPS and reduce the latency, when the Send Rate does not reach a threshold, we can appropriately reduce the size of the batchsize. When Send Rate exceeds the threshold, we need to choose a larger batchsize to increase the TPS and reduce the latency. Matching batchsize with Send Rate can better improve Fabric's performance. At the same time, we noticed that the CPU resource utilization efficiency was very poor during the experiment. Therefore, improving the CPU utilization mechanism inside Fabric is also a feasible solution to improve TPS.

5.3 Hyperledger Sawtooth's Performance

For Sawtooth, we first select Sawtooth 1.0.5 as the test benchmark. By modifying the protocol buffer and sawtooth-sdk version levels listed as dependencies in *packages/caliper-sawtooth/package.json* in caliper, then rebuild the Caliper project and test. We prepare "query" and "smallbank" workloads for Sawtooth. The "smallbank" workload includes transaction savings, deposit checking, send payment, write check, and amalgamate operations. We set txNumber to 500, 500, the number of accounts in smallbank to 30, the number of transactions per block to 10, and then test. The results show that with the increase of the Send Rate, the TPS of the "query" workload also increases. For the "smallbank" workload, a bottleneck occurs when the throughput reaches about 44 (see Fig. 11). In terms of latency, the latency of "query" can be ignored, and the latency of "smallbank" will continue to increase with the increase of the Send Rate. The initial period will show a linear growth trend. When the Send Rate is too high, it will show an exponential growth trend (see Fig. 12). Then we adjust the number of transactions per block.

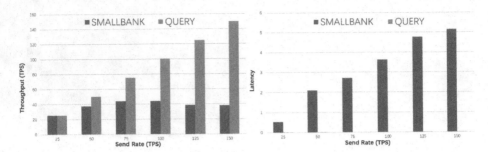

Fig. 11. Throughput of Sawtooth with varying workload.

Fig. 12. Latency of Sawtooth with varying workload.

Discussion: Through testing, we found that increasing the number of transactions per block within a certain range can increase TPS. When the number of transactions per block is set to 2000, the TPS can reach about 2000. In terms of consensus algorithms, sawtooth supports a variety of consensus algorithms, such as PBFT, PoET [15], Raft, etc. With the continuous improvement of consensus algorithms, the performance of sawtooth will also be improved. In terms of performance, the development team spent a lot of energy to migrate the core components of Sawtooth from Python to Rust. As the migration work is gradually completed, the performance of sawtooth will be further improved.

5.4 Fisco-Bcos's Performance

For Fisco-Bcos, we first deploy our own Fisco-Bcos network. Then we add a new network configuration file and create a test script that includes initialization, run, and end phases. Finally, we add the new test script as a test round to the test profile, ensuring that the correct callback was specified for Caliper. We prepare two basic workloads "set" and "get" for Fisco-Bcos. "Set" is responsible for generating a "hello world" smart contract and deploying this smart contract. "Get" is responsible for calling the smart contract and outputting "hello world". We set txNumber to 5000, 5000, and then test. The results show that with the increase of the Send Rate, the TPS of the "get" workload increases linearly, while the TPS of the "set" workload will reach the bottleneck around 1500 (see Fig. 13). For the latency, the latency of the "set" and "get" workloads hardly changes with the Send Rate. The latency of the "set" workload is slightly higher than the "get" workload, and the "get" workload has almost no latency (see Fig. 14).

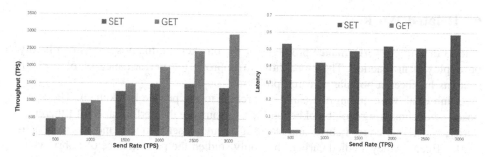

Fig. 13. Throughput of Fisco-Bcos with varying workload.

Fig. 14. Latency of Fisco-Bcos with varying workload.

Discussion: Fisco-Bcos is mainly optimized in terms of network transmission models and computing storage processes which provides great help for performance improvement. In terms of architecture, from the perspectives of storage, networking, and computing, Fisco-Bcos is upgraded around high availability and high ease-using. At the same time, based on the design principles of modularity, tiering, and pluggability, Fisco-Bcos continues to reshape the core modules to ensure the robustness of the system.

5.5 Comparison Analysis

By comparing the four blockchain systems, we can find that in a general setup, the TPS of Ethereum is significantly lower than the other three systems. The performance of Fabric is much better than Ethereum, but under our test conditions, it is far from the theoretical value of Fabric performance. The TPS of Sawtooth and Fisco-Bcos is better than the Fabric, which is also the consortium blockchain.

In terms of latency, the average latency of Ethereum and Fabric will be slightly larger, the average latency of Sawtooth will be smaller, and the average latency of Fisco-Bcos is the smallest (see Table 2). Due to the test platform limitation, we may not be able to measure the theoretical peak performance of the blockchain system. At the same time, because the architecture and functions of the blockchain system are not the same, we cannot use a relatively uniform workload. Therefore, the experimental results can be used as a reference.

Table 2. Performance comparison of 4 blockchain systems in our testing environment

	TPS	Latency
Ethereum	10–30	5 s
Fabric	100–200	1–10 s
Sawtooth	500–2000	0.5–5 s
Fisco-Bcos	1500–3000	0.5 s

6 Related Work

Due to the current performance problems of the blockchain, many systems can hardly be deployed in practice. Therefore, how to improve the performance of blockchain systems has been a popular research problem.

Dinh et al. were among the early researchers to the private blockchain. They proposed a benchmarking tool, blockbench [16], to compare the performance of Ethereum, Parity, and Hyperledger Fabric, and tested it through a set of micro and macro benchmarks. Because they studied earlier, they only studied the performance of Fabric v0.6.

Thakkar et al. conducted some research on Hyperledger Fabric v1.0, tested Fabric by adjusting configuration parameters, and proposed some simple optimization schemes based on the test results [17]. The current Fabric v1.4 architecture has many improvements compared to the old version, so many of their conclusions need to be reexamined in the new version.

Gorenflo et al. changed the fabric's architecture to reduce the calculation and I/O overhead during transaction sequencing and verification, thereby increasing the throughput from 3,000 to 20,000 [29].

Pongnumkul et al. compared the performance of Ethereum and Fabric, but the workload they choose a bit single [18]. Rouhani et al. analyzed the performance of two Ethereum clients, Geth and Parity [19]. Ampel et al. analyzed the performance of Sawtooth and identified some potential problems [20]. Hao et al. studied the impact of consensus algorithms on the performance of private blockchains [21].

Hyperledger Caliper is a blockchain performance benchmark framework, which allows users to test different blockchain solutions with predefined use cases and get a set of performance test results. This project is developing rapidly, and currently supports many projects in Hyperledger, and it is still expanding.

The development of the blockchain system is fast, and many past studies can no longer serve as a reasonable reference. At the same time, many new blockchain platforms are constantly appearing. Therefore, we need to conduct a new evaluation of the current mainstream blockchain system performance.

7 Conclusion and Future Work

In this work, we firstly analyzed the architecture of Ethereum, Hyperledger Fabric, Hyperledger Sawtooth and Fisco-Bcos in detail. Then we used the Hyperledger caliper as the benchmark tool and tested these blockchain systems in detail. We take transaction throughput and latency as the main performance metrics, install test tool in the blockchain systems, deploy smart contracts according to the information specified in the configuration, and start monitoring objects to monitor the resource consumption of the backend blockchain system. According to our defined workloads, the test tool will test the blockchain systems. A comprehensive analysis of the performance of the blockchain system was made by adjusting parameters such as Send Rate and batchsize, and finally the results were obtained. Based on the analysis results, we give some possible performance optimization schemes. We can see that the performance gap between the public blockchain and the consortium blockchain is very large. Therefore,

Ethereum needs to develop a new generation as soon as possible to improve their performance. For Fabric, as one of the most concerned members in the consortium blockchains, its performance is not as good as the emerging consortium blockchains. Sawtooth is also an open source distributed ledger platform. It is also used to run smart contracts and aims at digital financial asset management. The overall architecture is clear and highly modular, so the ability to customize is also strong. Fisco-Bcos is derived from the Ethereum C++ version. After years of development, major changes have been made in terms of scalability, performance, and ease-using. Fisco-Bcos 2.0 has added a group architecture to overcome the bottleneck of system throughput and its performance is very good.

There are still many shortcomings in this experiment. Due to the configuration of the experimental environment, the performance we get is far from the theoretical performance. In terms of workloads, we have only a few types of workloads that make it impossible to perform a complete assessment of the performance of the entire blockchain system.

In the future, we plan to use cloud services to conduct larger-scale experiments. We will continue to study the performance optimization methods of blockchain systems, and at the same time add consensus algorithms to our research direction. In addition, we will conduct more in-depth research on the architecture of the blockchain systems to improve the performance of the blockchain systems.

Acknowledgment. This work is supported by Key-Area Research and Development Program of Guangdong Province (NO. 2020B010164003), National Natural Science Foundation of China (No. 61702492), Shenzhen Basic Research Program (No. JCYJ20170818153016513), Shenzhen Discipline Construction Project for Urban Computing and Data Intelligence, Science and Technology Development Fund of Macao S.A.R (FDCT) under number 0015/2019/AKP, and Youth Innovation Promotion Association CAS.

References

1. Nakamoto, S.: Bitcoin: A peer-to-peer electronic cash system. https://bitcoin.org/bitcoin.pdf. Accessed 9 Jan 2020
2. Ethereum blockchain app platform. https://www.ethereum.org/. Accessed 9 Jan 2020
3. The Linux Foundation Homepage. https://www.linuxfoundation.org/. Accessed 9 Jan 2020
4. Hyperledger Homepage. https://www.hyperledger.org/. Accessed 9 Jan 2020
5. Hyperledger Fabric Homepage. https://www.hyperledger.org/projects/fabric. Accessed 9 Jan 2020
6. Hyperledger Sawtooth Homepage. https://www.hyperledger.org/projects/sawtooth. Accessed 9 Jan 2020
7. Fisco-Bcos Homepage. http://www.fisco-bcos.org/. Accessed 9 Jan 2020
8. Jakobsson, M., Juels, A.: Proofs of work and bread pudding protocols (extended abstract). In: Preneel, B. (ed.) Secure Information Networks. ITIFIP, vol. 23, pp. 258–272. Springer, Boston, MA (1999). https://doi.org/10.1007/978-0-387-35568-9_18
9. King, S., Nadal, S.: Ppcoin: Peer-to-peer crypto-currency with proof-of-stake. Self-published paper, vol. 19 (2012)
10. Castro, M., Liskov, B.: Practical Byzantine fault tolerance. OSDI **99**, 173–186 (1999)

11. Ongaro, D., Ousterhout, J.: In search of an understandable consensus algorithm. In: 2014 USENIX Annual Technical Conference (USENIX ATC 2014), pp. 305–319 (2014)
12. Docker Homepage. https://www.docker.com/. Accessed 9 Jan 2020
13. Demers, A., et al.: Epidemic algorithms for replicated database maintenance. ACM SIGOPS Oper. Syst. Rev. **22**(1), 8–32 (1988)
14. Hyperledger Caliper Homepage. https://hyperledger.github.io/caliper/. Accessed 9 Jan 2020
15. Level DB Database Homepage. https://github.com/a/leveldb. Accessed 9 Jan 2020
16. Dinh, T.T.A., et al.: Blockbench: a framework for analyzing private blockchains. In: Proceedings of the 2017 ACM International Conference on Management of Data, pp. 1085–1100. ACM (2017)
17. Thakkar, P., Nathan, S., Viswanathan. B.: Performance benchmarking and optimizing hyperledger fabric blockchain platform. In: 2018 IEEE 26th International Symposium on Modeling, Analysis, and Simulation of Computer and Telecommunication Systems (MASCOTS), pp. 264–276. IEEE (2018)
18. Pongnumkul, S., Siripanpornchana, C., Thajchayapong, S.: Performance analysis of private blockchain platforms in varying workloads. In: 2017 26th International Conference on Computer Communication and Networks (ICCCN), pp. 1–6. IEEE (2017)
19. Rouhani, S., Deters, R.: Performance analysis of ethereum transactions in private blockchain. In: 2017 8th IEEE International Conference on Software Engineering and Service Science (ICSESS), pp. 70–74. IEEE (2017)
20. Ampel, B., Patton, M., Chen, H.: Performance Modeling of Hyperledger Sawtooth Blockchain. In: 2019 IEEE International Conference on Intelligence and Security Informatics (ISI), pp. 59–61. IEEE (2019)
21. Hao, Y., et al.: Performance analysis of consensus algorithm in private blockchain. In: 2018 IEEE Intelligent Vehicles Symposium (IV), pp. 280–285. IEEE (2018)
22. Chaincodes. http://hyperledger-fabric.readthedocs.io/en/release-1.1/chaincode4noah.html. Accessed 9 Jan 2020
23. Membership Service Providers (MSP). http://hyperledger-fabric.readthedocs.io/en/release-1.1/msp.html. Accessed 9 Jan 2020
24. Node SDK for Fabric Client/Application. https://github.com/hyperledger/fabric-sdk-node. Accessed 9 Jan 2020
25. Omohundro, S.: Cryptocurrencies, smart contracts, and artificial intelligence. AI Matters **1**(2), 19–21 (2014)
26. Yan, Y., Zheng, K., Guo, Z.: Ethereum Technical Details and Actual Combat, 1st edn. China Machine Press, Beijing (2018)
27. On sharding blockchains. https://github.com/ethereum/wiki/wiki/Sharding-FAQ. Accessed 9 Jan 2020
28. Barger, A., et al.: Scalable communication middleware for permissioned distributed ledgers. In: Proceedings of the 10th ACM International Systems and Storage Conference, p. 1, May 2017
29. Gorenflo, C., et al.: FastFabric: scaling hyperledger fabric to 20,000 transactions per second. In: 2019 IEEE International Conference on Blockchain and Cryptocurrency (ICBC), pp. 455–463. IEEE (2019)
30. Chen, L., Xu, L., Shah, N., Gao, Z., Lu, Y., Shi, W.: On security analysis of proof-of-elapsed-time (PoET). In: Spirakis, P., Tsigas, P. (eds.) SSS 2017. LNCS, vol. 10616, pp. 282–297. Springer, Cham (2017). https://doi.org/10.1007/978-3-319-69084-1_19

Short Paper Track

Midiag: A Sequential Trace-Based Fault Diagnosis Framework for Microservices

Lun Meng[1], Yao Sun[2], and Shudong Zhang[3(✉)]

[1] College of Public Administration, Hohai University, Nanjing 210098, China
m_l_01@163.com
[2] Nanjing Institute of Big Date, Jinling Institute of Technology,
Nanjing 211169, China
suny216@jit.edu.cn
[3] Information Engineering College, Capital Normal University,
Beijing 100048, China
zsd@cnu.edu.cn

Abstract. Cloud applications are often deployed in shared data centers to optimize resource allocation and improve management efficiency. However, since a cloud application often has a large amount of different microservices, it is difficult for operators to analyze these microservices with a unified model. To deal with the above problem, this paper proposes a sequential trace-based fault diagnosis framework called as Midiag by mining the patterns of microservices' system call sequences. Midiag collects system calls with a non-invasive light-weight tool, and then uses k-means to cluster system call sequences as patterns with the longest common subsequence. The GRU-based neural network is employed to model the patterns of system call sequences to predict the next system call, and thus we can diagnose faults by comparing the predicted next system call and the actual next one in the specific pattern. We have validated Midiag with many different types of applications deployed in containers. The results demonstrate that Midiag can well classify these applications as different types and accurately diagnose the injected faults.

Keywords: Fault diagnosis · System call · Microservices · Cloud applications

1 Introduction

Microservice architectures is increasingly used to develop various applications due to its advantages such as efficient development, quick deployment and flexible scaling. In recent years, software applications based on a microservice architecture have been widely deployed in cloud computing data centers, and their infrastructures (e.g. Kubernetes, Mesos) have also developed rapidly to support and manage large-scale microservices. As various microservice applications have different resource requirements and behavior characteristics, the operators of a data center pay much more attention to the management strategies of microservices. A microservice architecture includes heterogeneous software, e.g., open-source software, third-party services and application-specific software. Analyzing and understanding microservice-based applications is the key to ensure

Q. Wang et al. (Eds.): SCC 2020, LNCS 12409, pp. 137–144, 2020.
https://doi.org/10.1007/978-3-030-59592-0_9

applications' reliability. Existing methods usually study the attributes of a single service or application, e.g., executable file name, port number, file metadata. However, these attributes are not the inherent attributes of microservices, which can be dynamically adjusted or hidden with operation and maintenance. Thus, the application-specific analysis cannot dynamically adapt to changing cloud computing. Some tools inspect packets, but analyzing the runtime behavior of deployed microservices has much overhead. Furthermore, these tools cannot accurately analyze the characteristics of microservices in the code level. Moreover, the strict privacy policy of cloud computing prohibits the intrusive analysis of microservices, which increases the difficulty of profiling microservices.

To address the above challenges, this paper proposes a sequential trace-based fault diagnosis framework for microservices called as Midiag. We collect sequential system calls to trace the runtime behaviors of various microservices with a unified, efficient and non-invasive way, when microservices interact with the host operating system, e.g., accessing file systems, synchronizing threads. Then, we employ k-means to cluster the collected sequential system calls as sequence patterns with Longest Common Subsequence (LCS). Finally, we employ the GRU-based neural network to model a sequence pattern, predict the next system call, and then diagnose faults by comparing the expected system call and the actual one in the specific pattern.

2 Related Work

Monitoring technologies are the basis of fault diagnosis by identifying the deviations from normal system behaviors. Existing works have proposed many models for fault diagnosis, such as subsequence analysis [1], behavioral Markov model [2], finite state automata [3], dynamic Bayesian network [4], and deep neural network [5]. Ref. [6] proposes a mandatory security policy generated by normal application behaviors in the system call level, which can realize simple admission controls regardless of the dependency of cross-system call sequences. The above method is limited to network-based applications and their communication protocols [7], while Midiag is generally applicable for various applications. Ref. [8] and [9] propose outlier detection methods based on semi-supervised learning (e.g., clustering) with labeled and unlabeled samples. The above methods are suitable for small-scale systems, but they are difficult to deal with the actual deployment scenarios of applications with various microservices and complex dependencies [10]. Midiag diagnoses faults by automatically analyzing system calls without applications' domain knowledge.

3 Midiag Design

Figure 1 shows the system architecture of Midiag, which includes trace collector, trace pattern miner, microservice modeler and fault diagnostor.

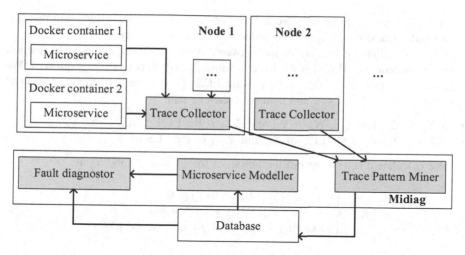

Fig. 1. Midiag system architecture

3.1 Trace Collector

We deploy a trace collector in every host to collect the traces of Docker containers deployed in the host. The trace collector employs a kernel virtualization tool that is IO Visor (https://github.com/iovisor) to collect the kernel events of interest without customizing the kernel by dynamically injecting user-defined bytecodes into kernel hook functions. IO Visor combines open source components to build networking, security and tracing in datacenters. We adopt bcc that is a component of IO Visor supporting immediate compilation to allow IO Visor programs running at the host speed in kernel. When a microservice is loaded, the Docker container notifies the daemon of the user space with PID, and the trace collector starts to collect system calls. The collector monitors the system calls of every microservices deployed on an operating system; the trace collector registers the PIDs of monitored Docker containers in the PID table; the trace collector sends the system call sequences of microservices registered in the PID table to the trace pattern miner for further mining trace patterns.

3.2 Trace Pattern Miner

Microservices carry out a series of activities by invoking system calls. Since different microservices have various system call patterns, we classifying microservices with similar system call sequences for improving the accuracy of fault diagnosis. The system calls collected from the trace collector are stored in the database for persistent storage, and the trace pattern miner employs k-means to cluster system call sequences with historical traces. In the training stage, the trace pattern miner clusters the system call sequences collected from the trace collectors as k microservice types with k-means. In the testing stage, the trace pattern miner takes a test system call sequence collected from a trace collector as an input, and then selects the cluster with the highest similarity as its microservice type. Trace pattern miner measures the similarities between the system call sequence to be detected and the central points of k clusters, and then the most similar microservice type is regarded as its microservice type.

First, we calculate the similarity between system call sequences. The longest common subsequence (LCS) is the longest subsequences between two sequences. We suppose that sequence $Z = (z_1, z_2,...,z_k)$ is the LCS of sequence $X = (x_1, x_2,...,x_m)$ and sequence $Y = (y_1, y_2,...,y_n)$, and then we conclude that:

- If $X_m = Y_n$, then $Z_k = X_m = Y_n$, and Z_{k-1} is the LCS of X_{m-1} and Y_{n-1};
- If $X_m \neq Y_n$, Z_k is the LCS of X_m and Y_{n-1} or the LCS of X_{m-1} and Y_n.

We calculate c [i, j] to record the length of the LCS of X_i and Y_j as:

$$c[i,j] = \begin{cases} 0, i = 0 \, or \, j = 0 \\ c[i-1,j-1]+1, i,j > 0 \, and \, x_i = y_i \\ max(c[i,j-1], c[i-1,j]), i,j > 0 \, and \, x_i \neq y_i \end{cases}.$$

The LCS of X and Y can be recursively performed in the following way:

- When $x_m = y_n$, we calculate the LCS of X_{m-1} and Y_{n-1}, and then add x_m or y_n to the tail to obtain the LCS of X and Y.
- When $x_m \neq y_n$, we calculate the LCS of X_{m-1} and Y and the LCS of X and Y_{n-1}.

After obtaining the system call sequence of each microservice, we calculate the distance between two system call sequences, and then use the distance to measure the similarity between system call sequences as:

$$D(X,Y) = 1 - \frac{|lcs(X,Y)|}{|X| + |Y| - |lcs(X,Y)|}$$

where |X| and |Y| are the lengths of system call sequence X and that of the system call sequence Y, and lcs(X,Y) is the LCS between X and Y. If X and Y are exactly the same, then d(x, y) = 0; if X and Y have no common subsequence, then d(x, y) = 1.

With the distance between the system call sequences and patterns, we cluster microservices' system call sequences, so that the microservices' system call patterns can be categorized to improve the accuracy of fault diagnosis. The k-means method firstly randomly finds a representative system call sequence for each cluster, and respectively assigns other objects to respective clusters according to the distances between them and the representative of clusters. If replacing a cluster representative with a new object can improve the quality of the obtained cluster, the representative of the cluster can be replaced with a new one. System call sequences can be classified into k different categories after iterations.

3.3   Microservice Modeler

We take system call sequences as the input of GRU neural networks with the attention mechanism to train GRU neural networks, and then obtain the trained GRU neural network, where each neural network pattern corresponds to a type of system call sequences. k GRU neural network patterns are respectively established for k types of microservices' system call sequences. We construct a GRU-based neural network model for each system call pattern as follows.

The first (n−1) system calls of the corresponding system call sequences are encoded as the hidden variables of a neural network's input layer. The hidden variables present context variables containing data flow information of the whole system call sequence. The attention mechanism is employed to allocate weight coefficients to the hidden variables. The more layers a network has, the stronger ability to learn and predict system call sequences it has. However, when the number of layers is too high, the training of the pattern is difficult to converge, so we employ a 3-layer GRU network. We add a full connection layer at the end to reduce the output's dimension. The Softmax function is used as the output layer of the neural network, and the corresponding tag is the category of system call sequence. The neural network pattern is trained with the gradient descent and the back-propagation loss, the parameters of the pattern are continuously adjusted, and then the trained GRU-based neural network pattern is obtained.

3.4   Fault Diagnostor

The similarities between the system call sequence to be detected with the representative sequences of k clusters are measured. We first classify a system call sequence as the cluster with the greatest similarity. For each cluster, we train a GRU-based model with the dataset of system call sequences. The original input sequence is reconstructed into a variable vector, and the fault diagnosis is carried out on the newly added sequence. The input sequence is converted into an encoding vector before being input into the GRU-based model. The output of the GRU layer is repeated S times to construct an intermediate sequence, where S is the length of the input sequence. The intermediate sequence passes through a time distribution dense layer with a Softmax activation function, and then the sequence is decoded as an original input sequence by another GRU layer.

The system call sequence to be detected is the input of the GRU neural network built in the specific cluster. The difference between the predicted system call and the actual one is measured as the abnormality degree. After the last system call is removed from the system call sequence, the system call sequence is used as the input of the GRU neural network trained in the corresponding cluster. The pattern encodes this system call sequence as a hidden variable, and generates the hidden variable into a context variable containing data flow information with the attention mechanism. GRU predicts the category of the next system call in the system call sequence, and outputs the normalized discrete probability distribution through the Softmax function. The Manhattan distance is used to calculate the difference between the probability distribution vector of the next system call predicted by the GRU neural network and the vector of the next actual system call. The distance is taken as an anomaly degree, where the larger the distance is, the larger the anomaly degree of the system call is.

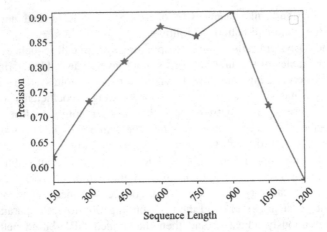

Fig. 2. System call sequence length on precision

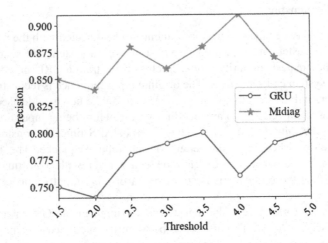

Fig. 3. Fault diagnosis threshold on precision

4   Evaluation

The experimental environment includes eight virtual machines (VMs) running on Ubuntu 18; each VM has a 2.40 GHz virtual CPU core and 32 GB memory; each VM employs bcc and JIT to collect system calls.

This section evaluates Midiag with precision that is the ratio of correctly detected faults and injected faults in ref. [11]. We choose sixteen microservices categorized as SQL database (i.e., PostgreSQL, Ingres r3, MaxDB, InterBase), NoSQL database (i.e., MongoDB, Cassandra, HBASE, Memcache), Web server (i.e., Apache, Nginx, Lighttpd, Appweb), FTP client (i.e., File Zilla, Fire FTP, gFTP, LFTP). To train the GRU-based model, we collect one thousand system call sequences for each microservice. A single GRU-based model is trained with the dataset of system call sequences generated by all microservices, and then a sample is detected with the unified model. Furthermore, Midiag trains multiple GRU-based models with multiple datasets of system call sequences generated by microservices in different clusters, respectively. If the loss returned by the GRU-based model is higher than the threshold, the detected sample is detected as a fault. Each experiment is repeated 100 times.

Firstly, we evaluate the length of system call sequence on precision. Figure 2 shows that the longer the length is, the more accurate the precision is, before the threshold of the sequence length reaches 900, and Midiag can achieve the best precision 0.91. However, the precision decreases after that, because the longer sequence causes the overfit of the trained model. Secondly, we compare Midiag with the traditional single GRU-based model. Figure 3 shows the effect of loss threshold on the accuracy of fault diagnosis. If the threshold is too high, more faults of system call sequence will be classified as normal (i.e., false negative). If the threshold is too low, the normal sequence will be incorrectly classified as abnormal (i.e., false positive). The achievable accuracy of a single GRU-based model is less than 0.80, while Midiag can achieve precision 0.91 by categorizing sixteen microservices as five clusters and diagnosing faults in each cluster according to the cluster of system call sequences.

5   Conclusion

The microservice architecture raises great challenges to the operation and maintenance of applications in cloud computing. Existing operation technologies usually employ a unified model to analyze applications' status. However, the behaviors of various microservices vary greatly, and describing them with a single model is difficult. To address the above issue, this paper proposes a microservice fault diagnosis framework Midiag based on mining system call patterns. After collecting system calls with a non-invasive lightweight tool, we employ k-means to cluster system call sequences as sequence patterns with LCS. The GRU-based neural network is adopted to model a sequence pattern to predict the future system call, and thus we can detect faults by comparing the predicted system call and the actual one in a specific pattern. Experimental results show that Midiag can effectively distinguishes system call sequences and achieve much higher precision in detecting faults.

Acknowledgment. This work is supported by National Key R&D Program of China (2018YFB1402900).

References

1. Forrest, S., Hofmeyr, S., Somayaji, A.: The evolution of system call collecting. In: The Annual Computer Security Applications Conference, Piscataway, NJ, pp. 418–430. IEEE Computer Society (2008). https://doi.org/10.1109/acsac.2008.54
2. Maggi, F., Matteucci, M., Zanero, S.: Detecting intrusions through system call sequence and argument analysis. IEEE Trans. Dependable Secure Comput. 7(4), 381–395 (2010). https://doi.org/10.1109/TDSC.2008.69

3. Sekar, R., Bendre, M., Dhurjati, D., Bollineni P.: A fast automaton based method for detecting anomalous program behaviors. In: Symposium on Security and Privacy, Piscataway, NJ, pp. 144–155. IEEE Computer Society (2001). https://doi.org/10.1109/secpri.2001.924295

4. Fenga, L., Guana, X., Guoa, S., Gaoa, Y., Liua, P.: Predicting the intrusion intentions by observing system call sequences. Comput. Secur. **23**(3), 241–252 (2004). https://doi.org/10.1016/j.cose.2004.01.016

5. Kolosnjaji, B., Zarras, A., Webster, G., Eckert, C.: Deep learning for classification of malware system call sequences. In: Kang, B.H., Bai, Q. (eds.) AI 2016. LNCS (LNAI), vol. 9992, pp. 137–149. Springer, Cham (2016). https://doi.org/10.1007/978-3-319-50127-7_11

6. Provos., N.: Improving host security with system call policies. In: the 12th Conference on USENIX Security Symposium, Berkeley, pp. 1–18. USENIX (2003). 10.1.1.13.2425

7. Bernaille, L., Teixeira, R., Salamatian, K.: Early application identification. In: ACM CoNEXT Conference, New York, NY, USA, pp. 1–12. ACM (2006). https://doi.org/10.1145/1368436.1368445

8. Ermana, J., Mahanti, A., Arlitt, M., Cohen, I., Williamson, C.: Offline/realtime traffic classification using semi-supervised learning. Perform. Eval. **64**(9), 1194–1213 (2007). https://doi.org/10.1016/j.peva.2007.06.014

9. Zhang, J., Chen, X., Xiang, Y., Zhou, W., Wu, J.: Robust network traffic classification. IEEE/ACM Trans. Netw. **23**(4), 1257–1270 (2015). https://doi.org/10.1109/TNET.2014.2320577

10. Jamshidi, P., Pahl, C., Mendonca, N.C., Lewis, J., Tilkov, S.: Microservices: the journey so far and challenges ahead. IEEE Softw. **35**(3), 24–35 (2018). https://doi.org/10.1109/MS.2018.2141039

11. Magalhes, J.P., Silva, L.M.: SHoWA: a self-healing framework for web-based applications. ACM Trans. Auton. Adapt. Syst. **10**(1), 1–28 (2015). https://doi.org/10.1145/2700325

An Empirical Study of Web API Quality Formulation

Esi Adeborna[1] and Kenneth K. Fletcher[2]($\boxtimes$) (iD)

[1] University of Massachusetts Lowell, Lowell, MA 01854, USA
esi_adeborna@student.uml.edu
[2] University of Massachusetts Boston, Boston, MA 02125, USA
kenneth.fletcher@umb.edu

Abstract. This paper presents an empirical study on one of the most popular web API repositories, www.programmableweb.com. The study is to ascertain the impact of the structure and formulation of external web API quality factors on the overall web API quality. The study is based on the hypothesis that, in such a multi-factor quality measurement, the structure and formulation of the quality factors can make a substantial difference in its quantification. Specifically, we employ statistical tools such as exploratory factor analysis, to determine the latent factors that contributes to web API quality. We subsequently determine the loading of each latent factors to propose a new quality model for web API quality computation.

Keywords: Web API · Web API quality · Web API quality factors · Factor analysis · Mashup development

1 Introduction

Web Application Programming Interfaces (APIs) have become increasingly prevalent in recent past as they provide a platform that allows other applications to interact and request for data or use their functionality. With this many web APIs, typically with similar functionality, it becomes challenging to select or recommend web APIs to meet users' needs. Therefore, in order to provide a distinction among functionally similar web APIs, quality factors are used [1,2].

Web APIs, unlike web services, hide their internal complexities and internal details. Therefore they depend on external factors to drive their suitability for integration into other applications [1,3,4]. According to the standard ISO/IEC 9126-1, external quality is based on a black box model and is related to the behavior of the software product in a given running environment [5]. Consequently, several API quality models, that depend on their external quality factors have been proposed [1,4,6]. In one of such quality models, proposed by Fletcher [1] which was an extension of Cappiello et al. [4], the quality of a web API depends on three quality dimensions, namely, *Functionality*, *Reliability* and *Usability*. This model was purely based on theoretical foundation and the behavior of web

© Springer Nature Switzerland AG 2020
Q. Wang et al. (Eds.): SCC 2020, LNCS 12409, pp. 145–153, 2020.
https://doi.org/10.1007/978-3-030-59592-0_10

APIs and as such has a couple limitations: (1) Their model assumes that all three quality dimensions contribute equally to the overall web API quality. This assumption equates the salience of each quality dimension in the web API Quality computation and therefore balances the Quality values of web APIs even if one dimension has increased salience than the others. (2) The formulation of the web API quality model does not take into consideration the correlation of the quality factors that make up the dimensions.

These limitations can lead to varied implications such as (1) inaccurate computation of low quality APIs as high quality, where low-quality web APIs could result in difficulty to integrate with other APIs and (2) cause developers to miss out on potentially quality web APIs because of inaccurate web API Quality values [1]. In this work, we propose a method to address the above limitations, by first performing an extensive empirical analysis of web API dataset using statistical parameters and exploratory factor analysis. We subsequently formulate a model for web API quality, based on results from our analysis.

2   Background on Web API Quality

Obtaining values of quality of service (QoS) parameters, such as availability, response time, etc. for web APIs is a challenging task because, web APIs typically hide their internal complexity and therefore external factors drive the evaluation of its quality computation [1,4]. For this reason, we adopt the quality model proposed by Fletcher [1] and Cappiello et al. [4], to define our black-box quality model for web APIs. This black-box quality model are organize along three main web API dimensions: (1) **Functionality:** considers the web API's *interoperability*, *compliance*, and *security* level [1]; (2) **Reliability:** measures the maturity of the web API by considering the available statistics of usage of the component together with the frequency of its changes and updates; and (3) **Usability:** A web API's usability is evaluated in terms of understandability by considering the available web API documentation by means of examples, API groups, blogs, sample source codes etc. [1].

3   Research Approach

This section first gives an overview of our approach and thereafter describes the main modules that drives our model. Our research study focuses on a series of statistical analysis to determine the content and distribution of the variables of interest to accurately compute the quality of a web API. We develop the conceptual and mathematical underpinnings of the proposed quality model and finally propose a web API quality model based on results of our statistical analysis.

3.1   Dataset Description

Our empirical study focuses on studying one of the popular online web APIs repository, www.programmableweb.com. This is by far the largest online web

Table 1. Top 5 Web API categories from programmableweb.com

Category	Number of Web APIs
Tools	787
Financial	583
Enterprise	486
eCommerce	434
Social	402

API repository that contains approximately 23,000 web APIs, with various functionalities [3,7]. We study a version of this data, API dataset [1], which was crawled from www.programmableweb.com in March 2018. This dataset contains 12,879 web API records with 383 categories. Table 1 shows a list of the top 5 categories in the dataset. Each web API in our dataset is described by 19 fields such as name, description, authentication model, request and response formats, etc.

3.2 Empirical Study

To explore the content and the distribution of our dataset, we performed a series of statistical analysis. In our analysis, we focus on the external variables that define the quality of a web API. Table 2 presents central tendency of web API dataset variables of interest and dispersion within the variables' distribution. Due to the great numeric range in the dataset on these different variables, we normalize the values for the variables of interest.

Noteworthy findings are that, most of the web APIs have almost no *SDKs* as revealed in its average and median for 0.15 and 0 respectively. In addition, the *SDKs* are highly skewed to the right of the distribution around the mean. *How-tos* and *Sample API Codes* have a similar and largely skewed distribution as *SDK*, with mean values almost zero. There is a relatively better distribution for *API Versions* than the previous variables with a mean and median almost

Table 2. Descriptive statistics for the external quality variables (N = 12,879)

	Mean	SD	Median	Range	Skew
SDKs	0.15	0.36	0.00	1.00	1.97
How-tos	0.01	0.09	0.00	1.00	11.45
Sample Codes	0.10	0.30	0.00	1.00	2.70
API Versions	0.70	0.14	0.74	0.88	−2.60
API Languages	0.42	0.06	0.42	0.50	0.82
Data Formats	0.80	0.40	1.00	1.00	−1.47
Security	0.36	0.20	0.40	0.80	1.29

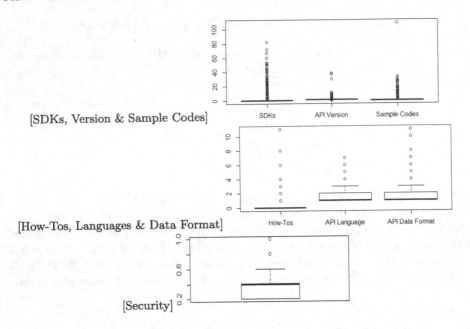

[SDKs, Version & Sample Codes]

[How-Tos, Languages & Data Format]

[Security]

Fig. 1. Boxplots of the web API external variables

Table 3. Pearson correlation between web API external variables (N = 12,879)

	(1)	(2)	(3)	(4)	(5)	(6)	(7)
(1) SDKs	–						
(2) How-tos	0.12	–					
(3) Sample codes	0.49	0.09	–				
(4) Reliability	0.02	0.02	0.05	–			
(5) Interoperability	0.23	0.06	0.19	0.02	–		
(6) Compliance	0.01	0.01	0.03	0.64	0.11	–	
(7) Security	−0.12	0.01	−0.02	0.10	−0.45	0.03	–

identical, and a standard deviation of 0.14. The highly skewed *API Versions* imply that most of the web APIs are updated regularly. This is an indication of good **reliability**, which measures the maturity of the web API by considering the frequency of its changes and updates. The number of different *API languages* show a distribution that is moderately skewed to the right, skew = 0.82. Typically, a web API is **compliant** if it supports at least one standard web API language. The *Data formats* external variable is negatively skewed with a standard deviation of 0.4, showing a wide dispersion around the mean. *Data formats* together with *API Languages* measures the **interoperability** of a web API. *Security* is positively skewed and has a smaller dispersion around the mean with a SD of 0.20. This indicates most of the web APIs have some kind of authentication system. Figure 1 shows the boxplots of the web API quality variables based on the API dataset.

3.3 Associations Between Web API External Variables

We employ Pearson Correlation (PC) matrix, to describe linear associations between the web API external variables. PC attempts to determine the amount of linear dependence between variables by describing their association as a straight line. Table 3 provides the results for the correlation between the variables. The values show a non-zero direct correlation between the variables with p-values less than 0.001. Our analysis of the correlation coefficients suggest the variables are weak to moderately correlated, mostly positive but negative for *Reliability* on *SDKs*, *Sample Code* and *Security*.

3.4 Exploratory Factor Analysis (EFA)

Exploratory Factor Analysis (EFA) is a statistical technique that is used to identify the latent relational structure among a set of variables [8]. Essentially, we use EFA to uncover the underlying structure of the relationship between the web API quality variables. First, we conduct parallel analysis scree plot to determine the acceptable number of factors. Figure 2 shows the scree plot of our parallel analysis. We locate the point of inflection (the point where the gap between simulated data and actual data tends to be minimum) to determine the minimum number of factors. In this case, it is 3.

Next we determined the factors to be extracted. We employ the oblique rotation based on the correlation between the variables. We used the "Ordinary Least Squared/Minres" factoring as it is known to provide results similar to "Maximum Likelihood" without assuming multivariate normal distribution and derives solutions through iterative eigen decomposition like principal axis [9, 10].

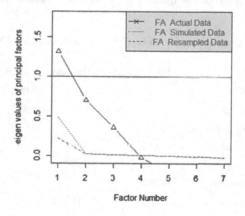

Fig. 2. EFA Parallel analysis scree plot

Using loadings of not less than absolute value of 0.3 [10], and not loading on more than one factor, Table 4 shows the results of our factor loading. With a factor of 3, our result produces a single-loading, also known as Simple Structure.

To validate the EFA for acceptable fit [9], we consider our Root Mean Square of Residuals (RMSR) from the result, which is 0. This is acceptable as the RMSR value for an acceptable fit should be closer to 0. Next we check the RMSEA (Root Mean Square Error of Approximation) index. Its value, 0.007 shows good model fit as it should be below 0.05. Finally, our Tucker-Lewis Index (TLI) is 0.99 - an acceptable value considering it's over 0.9. After establishing the adequacy of the factors, the EFA result was used as the basis for the proposed model, see Fig. 3.

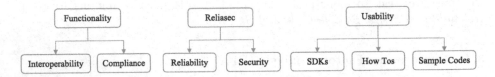

Fig. 3. Results of Factor Analysis of Web API variables

3.5   Web API Quality Formulation

Based on results from our analysis the following mathematical models have been proposed to define the web API quality dimensions. For each web API $w \in W$, there is a quality property $Q(w)$, that indicates the quality of the web API w given as:

$$Q(w) = 0.4 * Q_F(w) + 0.33 * Q_R(w) + 0.27 * Q_B(w) \qquad (1)$$

where Q_F, Q_R and Q_B are the quality dimensions for *Functionality* (F), *Reliasec* (R), and *Usability* (B) respectively. 0.4, 0.33 and 0.27 are the weight each quality dimension, *Functionality* (F), *Reliasec* (R), and *Usability* (B) respectively, contribute to the calculation of the quality of a web API. A new dimension, *Reliasec*,

Table 4. Factor loading for web API external variables (N = 12,879)

	Functionality	Reliasec	Usability
SDKs	–	–	0.609
How-tos	–	–	0.440
Sample codes	–	–	0.553
Reliability	0.816	–	–
Interoperability	–	0.837	–
Compliance	0.789	–	–
Security	–	−0.572	–

has been introduced and explained in Eq. (3). The formalized descriptions of the proposed web API Quality dimensions are as follows:

$$Q_F = \frac{1}{2}[(1 + \frac{|lang|}{k} + \frac{|dformat|}{l}) + 3comp] \tag{2}$$

where $lang$ and $dformat$ are the languages and data formats supported by the web API, and $comp$ is the compliance levels of the web API respectively.

$$Q_R = \frac{1}{2}[\frac{3}{5}sec + max\left(1 - \frac{cdate - ludate}{\frac{cdate-crdate}{|ver|}}, 0\right)] \tag{3}$$

where $cdate$, $ludate$, and $crdate$ are the current date, last use date and creation date of the web API respectively, and ver is the set of version available for that web API. sec is the security level of the web API. Based on our correlation matrix Sect. 3.3, *Security* and *Compliance* are highly correlated 0.64 than any of the other variables, which suggests they are similar measures for *Functionality*. Also, the factor analysis suggests the grouping of *Security* and *Reliability* into one factor, see Fig. 3. The mathematical Eq. (3), considers *Reliability* and *Security* in one dimension, namely *Reliasec*.

$$Q_B = \frac{1}{3}(sdks + how\_to + sample\_codes) \tag{4}$$

where $sdks$, how_tos, and $sample\_codes$ are number of SDKs, How-to Documentations and Sample Codes that are available for web API users.

We use Cronbach's alpha to validate the internal consistency of our proposed quality model in comparison to the existing model. Cronbach's alpha is a measure of internal consistency that indicates how closely related a set of items are as a group. The alpha values for the revised dimensions in the proposed models are 0.78 and 0.63 for functionality and reliasec respectively. These values are higher than the existing model of 0.51 and 0.46 for functionality and reliability.

4   Related Work

Web API quality research is minimal and the articles that focus on API quality have no emphasis on the effect of splitting web API attributes by weight in the multi-attribute measurement of web API quality. Bermbarch and Wittern [6] proposed an approach and a toolkit for benchmarking the quality of web APIs considering geo-mobility of clients. Their quality model comprises of two interconnected attributes namely, availability and performance. Volatile latency and temporary unavailability were considered quality problems without quantification of the role that each attribute plays in the quality of the web API.

Picozzi et al. [11] also proposed a quality model for mashup services. The Mashup quality computation, proposed in their work, considers the different roles mashup components play (i.e. master, slave and filter) that affect the perception of the quality of the final integration [11]. These roles, however, are not relevant to web APIs. Similarly, Fletcher [1] proposed a method that employs the black-box approach to analyze the quality of web APIs that match a mashup developer's requirement. Though his work recognized the need for web API quality computation based on its attributes, he computed web API quality as the normalized sum of its dimensions. This work intends to capitalize on this contribution but goes further to evaluate the multi-attribute measurement of web API quality.

In another research by Cappiello et al. [12], they address quality of mashups in the light of the activities that characterize their development process. They proposed evaluation techniques taking into account the constituent components of mashups. Their work supports our hypothesis but does not illustrate or validate the computation of the weights.

5   Conclusion

In this work, we proposed a reconfiguration of API quality computation model to promote increased accuracy in web API Quality calculations. This study uses Correlation to prove that, Security and Compliance are highly correlated, which suggests they are similar measures for Functionality. Exploratory Factor Analysis (EFA) suggests the grouping of Security and Reliability into one factor, in the Simple Structure. We have shown that our proposed model considers Reliability and Security in one dimension, which we name Reliasec. Also, this study uses EFA to examine how much weight each API quality dimensions contribute to API Quality. For future research, we would run more experiments to ascertain the performance of our model to increase accuracy in quality web API recommendations compared with other baseline methods.

References

1. Fletcher, K.K.: A quality-based web API selection for mashup development using affinity propagation. In: Ferreira, J.E., Spanoudakis, G., Ma, Y., Zhang, L.-J. (eds.) SCC 2018. LNCS, vol. 10969, pp. 153–165. Springer, Cham (2018). https://doi.org/10.1007/978-3-319-94376-3_10
2. Fletcher, K.K., Liu, X.F.: A collaborative filtering method for personalized preference-based service recommendation. In: 2015 IEEE International Conference on Web Services, pp. 400–407, June 2015
3. Fletcher, K.K.: A quality-aware web API recommender system for mashup development. In: Ferreira, J.E., Musaev, A., Zhang, L.-J. (eds.) SCC 2019. LNCS, vol. 11515, pp. 1–15. Springer, Cham (2019). https://doi.org/10.1007/978-3-030-23554-3_1
4. Cappiello, C., Daniel, F., Matera, M.: A quality model for mashup components. In: Gaedke, M., Grossniklaus, M., Díaz, O. (eds.) ICWE 2009. LNCS, vol. 5648, pp. 236–250. Springer, Heidelberg (2009). https://doi.org/10.1007/978-3-642-02818-2_19
5. ISO/IEC: ISO/IEC 25010: 2011 systems and software engineering-systems and software quality requirements and evaluation (square)-system and software quality models (2011)

6. Bermbach, D., Wittern, E.: Benchmarking web API quality. In: Bozzon, A., Cudre-Maroux, P., Pautasso, C. (eds.) ICWE 2016. LNCS, vol. 9671, pp. 188–206. Springer, Cham (2016). https://doi.org/10.1007/978-3-319-38791-8_11

7. Xia, B., Fan, Y., Tan, W., Huang, K., Zhang, J., Wu, C.: Category-aware API clustering and distributed recommendation for automatic mashup creation. IEEE Trans. Serv. Comput. 8(5), 674–687 (2015)

8. Child, D.: The Essentials of Factor Analysis. Cassell Educational, London (1990)

9. Hooper, D., Coughlan, J., Mullen, M.R.: Structural equation modelling: guidelines for determining model fit. Electron. J. Bus. Res. Methods 6(1), 53–60 (2008)

10. Kline, R.B.: Principles and Practice of Structural Equation Modeling, vol. 2. Guilford Press, New York City (2004)

11. Picozzi, M., Rodolfi, M., Cappiello, C., Matera, M.: Quality-based recommendations for mashup composition. In: Daniel, F., Facca, F.M. (eds.) ICWE 2010. LNCS, vol. 6385, pp. 360–371. Springer, Heidelberg (2010). https://doi.org/10.1007/978-3-642-16985-4_32

12. Cappiello, C., Matera, M., Picozzi, M., Daniel, F., Fernandez, A.: Quality-aware mashup composition: issues, techniques and tools. In: 2012 Eighth International Conference on the Quality of Information and Communications Technology, pp. 10–19. IEEE (2012)

Author Index

Printed in the United States
By Bookmasters